Asian Absences

Asian Absences

Searching for Shangri-La

by
Wolfgang Büscher

*Translated
by Simon Pare*

HAUS PUBLISHING
London

 ArmchairTraveller

Copyright © 2008 Wolfgang Büscher
Translation copyright © 2010 Simon Pare

First published in Great Britain in 2010 by
Haus Publishing Ltd,
70 Cadogan Place, London SW1X 9AH
www.hauspublishing.co.uk

Originally published under the title *Asiatische Absencen*
Copyright © 2008 by Rowohlt. Berlin Verlag GmbH, Berlin

The moral right of the author has been asserted

A CIP catalogue record for this book is available from the
British Library

ISBN 978-1-906598-76-1

Typeset in Garamond by MacGuru Ltd
Printed in the UK by J F Print Ltd., Sparkford, Somerset

For Anni

Contents

An Indian Afternoon

Nothing more now, at last. Only the cries of parrots through the open door, as if from far away – this room, its dusty silence, the camp bed I was lying on. How long had it been already? What time was it? Would my fellow travellers keep their word and come back? Questions that flickered and died.

I liked fever. I'd always liked it as a boy. Days in the house on my own. The ticking of the clock down in the dining-room, scrabbling under the floorboards, and the creaking of the beams, of the walls, like someone's teeth grinding in their sleep. Autumn had come. Stormy gusts lashed the house, but I lay in safety and listened to the rain and burrowed deeper into the book I'd been given to help me through the day, an Indian adventure. Under cover of darkness, one of my compatriots, a German ship's boy in Calcutta, fled the ship and its tyrannical captain. He was taken on by a group of Indian travelling mountebanks led by a cunning, avaricious dwarf who was not to be trusted. He did make friends with the elephant trainer, however. For the time being the boy was saved – we were saved, because I was completely involved and followed him into the depths of the country, into the strangest of the strange. What had been just a vague sense of unease tightened around him like a noose. The dwarf belonged to a secret cult that demanded victims, real victims of flesh and blood, not just rupees and grains of rice. The boy managed to escape again with the help of the elephant handler, but our hero was left behind, fatally wounded. I was burning when my mother found me with my fingers on the last page, whispering the name of the dying mahout. Indian fever, I heard our family doctor say. He had been a ship's doctor on the South Seas in his youth; now he bent over me with a strange smile, cooled my forehead and took my pulse. 'Sleep now, my boy. Sleep it off.'

I sat up and looked around the room – I'd heard the mumbling voice so clearly it was as if the old family doctor were sitting beside me on the camp bed. It wasn't possible. This was India, and the doctor was long dead. But where was my watch? Not on my wrist and not within reach either. Gone. Lost on the journey, on some dusty track or down some crack in the jeep. The jeep – my fellow travellers had brought me here in it when the fever came, and soon, soon I would remember everything, every detail of the journey, if only I could find my watch first. What time? When will they come and fetch me from here? Sleep, white man, sleep. Monkeys watch over you in your sleep, monkeys and parrots.

At some stage, I'd dozed off, woken up, dozed off again. The room lay in fading light, things cast weaker shadows, a last trace of the dwindling day fell through the doorway. The gecko hour, I thought to myself. But first a name crept forth, a beautiful, even elegant name, arching from one dark syllable to the next – Jodhpur.

We had come from Jodhpur – the photographer looking for pictures of India, an Indian friend who was driving us, an older man almost dwarf-like in size who had a business card with 'Professor' written on it and translated for us, and me with my notebook in my lap. We didn't have any specific plan, just an idea to drive from north to south, into a country full of gods. There was no avoiding them, the air was filled with offerings of incense and devotion; one Indian breath contained more religion than an entire German Advent. I drew it in and couldn't take my eyes off the rajput by the wayside, the boundless pride of a man from the warrior caste, silver rings on his bare feet. Nor off the spindly old woman. It was evening, she'd cut some branches for her animals. She was standing there, upright, her toes spread in the dust, the skin darker around her eyes, her arms thinner than the handle of the sickle she was leaning on like a hunter on his spear. I noticed how old she was and asked her what she still wished for in life. She gave me a look containing astonishment as well as contempt. 'Hari Bhavan!' she said, the house of God. Her eyes rejoiced. Soon he will call me from this body, from this dust, to him at last. The warrior and the old woman glowed, they appeared to see something that made them pay scant regard to things we would find grand or unbearable.

And then we were stuck in the bustle of a town, I spotted the god in the gutter. The heat lay over everything like a curse, and I was getting restless on the back seat of the jeep in a daze of exhaust fumes and smells. We weren't moving. Everyone was pushing, beeping, revving. Everything had come to a standstill. I pushed the door open and fanned it back and forth as hard as I could to make a draught, and then we had rolled forwards a few metres and Ganesh, the little elephant-headed god, appeared in the door frame. He was no bigger than my fist and was sitting in the fold between two root claws of an old roadside tree. Someone had built him a doll-sized temple that looked as if it had been abandoned after a children's game, and someone had woven him a tiny garland of flowers, which he wore around his tiny, thick elephant neck.

He looked anxious. His old eyes were wrinkled up as if he were troubled by something he could see coming. What could I do – scatter some flowers for him? I had none. His favourite food? I didn't know what it was. A few coins at least? I did nothing. I felt poor, useless, stupid. At last a tremor went through the mass of people and goods; it pushed and wrenched our jeep forwards. The little god vanished as suddenly as he had appeared.

We drifted more than we drove. The streets were rivers of bodies pressing onwards, never drying up, one cataract after another. I saw vehicles from every age, from the Bronze Age on, high-wheeled, hand-drawn carts alongside brand new vans, all of them decorated with pictures of gods and with the unnecessary request 'Please horn!' on the back. All of them beeped incessantly.

Out of the press of the city – I had got out and continued on foot – rose a high-pitched twittering, but it didn't sound like birdsong, it sounded metallic. I followed it and imagined a flock of futuristic birds, silver microchip-guided hummingbirds programmed for pleasure or for use in subtle warfare. Then, rounding the final corner, I saw them: it was the flock of writers, it was their square. They were sitting in their hundreds on the stone floor with short-legged tables in front of them on which their mechanical typewriters were waiting for customers. There were writers of petitions, of applications and requests of every imaginable kind, they drew up sales and marriage contracts and typed out the important letters whispered in their ear. From time to time, the chirruping that had attracted me would subside, only to start up again soon after – the many hundreds of keystrokes from all these typewriters. As I left, it flared up like a bush full of sparrows.

The next thing I saw was a naked beggar in the middle of the road, a thin, brown body exhibiting its grotesque deformities. The traffic divided and flowed smoothly around even his most effusive gestures. Everything pushed on and past. What was lying was left lying. Everyone steered his bus, his moped, his animal around the naked man, paying him no heed. Camels, people, donkeys harnessed to swaying, overloaded carts – the wheel of life was not an image, not a mystical idea, it was here. It turned ever onward, it pushed and shoved me, and if I wasn't careful, it would run me over as it had mercilessly run over so many before me, set in motion and kept in motion by wants and needs, dreams and desires, by muscles and thin sinews and burnt petrol, rotating ceaselessly on its old axis, grinding and grinding into ashes, into dust.

Only one species passed unharmed through the great noise, its languor a provocation – the sacred cow. As it made its way through the never-ending rush hour of bodies of metal and flesh, and the mire they left behind them, the cow's face always wore the same expression of sullen indifference, whether its lips were tearing off juicy green leaves or finding discarded leftovers of dal, the lentil dish. In their total lack of concern for how people looked at them, the holy cows were like the holy men who had at some stage left behind their families and everything else in their industrious lives to wander, clad in saffron robes or naked, for the rest of their days. They both passed through the world, no longer part of it.

The holy men lay in temples or amid icy peaks, smoking and mumbling ancient verses, inspired by one sole desire – not to have to go back after this life into the stream or under the wheel or into another skin that must hold together so many things that jostle and prick and seek to split apart. I had sat for a while with one near a village he had chosen as his summer home. He squatted there, smoked *bidis*, for the most part said nothing, and allowed himself to be fed by the villagers, who thought themselves lucky that such a holy bird, a sadhu, had winged its way to them. After a few hours, I had sat long enough, stood up and left. He took as little notice of this as he had of my arrival.

At some stage I noticed that the disgust had left me, disgust at India's smells, the sweet and the spicy, of rotting, excrement and decay, at the bright-red spit of the betel nut-chewers like spilt blood wherever you go. None of this assailed me anymore, my body no longer revolted at the repulsive aspects of this foreign land. And heat helped to fight India's heat; a ladleful of hot tea from the nearest roadside pan, milky-grey, gingery-hot, was enough. Ginger soothed the coughing caused by the exhaust fumes; the dose lasted until the next tea ambulance.

The indifference that met us in the cities was as great as the wide-eyed amazement we encountered in the villages. It wouldn't take a minute after our jeep had driven into one before the children discovered us. The jeep disappeared in the commotion like wild prey among a pride of young lions. It was a silent commotion. The gentle rustling of cotton-white clothes out of which a guttural word would suddenly rise and be answered by a high-pitched burst of laughter from the mob, then a sign from a precocious boy to be quiet would hush everything to a whisper again. They came up close. The jeep's window frames were filled with shy, curious children's faces.

Another village, more rustling and whispering of children. I didn't look, I just heard it as I dozed on the back seat. The rustling and whispering suddenly ceased. I sat up and looked into staring, red-streaked eyes in a dark, excited face, eyes that had nothing bright about them, only fever and delusion. We moved slowly forwards, the man keeping pace; he was clinging onto the jeep so hard, the white of his knuckles stood out. He stared, he didn't take his eyes off me.

He saw something that drove him mad. His aubergine-coloured lips opened to form a sound that never came. Was he mute? Haunted by visions? Or was he looking into a mirror, and I was that mirror? The jeep was standing still now, the heat was searing. My friends finally realized what has happening behind them; the jeep gave a roar, cleared a path for itself with its horn, accelerated. The man ran alongside, hanging into the open window, people stood back, as the jeep tore out of the village and shook off their stares. I thought of the family doctor: 'He has Indian fever.'

⤳

The next day I noticed that my temperature was rising. Everything was torment: the bumpy ride, the conversations, the miserable heat. I could hardly stand the last few hours in the jeep – the track jolted me badly, the humidity took my breath away. The betel spit when we stopped, blood everywhere. Ghee, ginger, curry, dal, everything merged into the thick smoke of the pyres by the river. No more warriors – thin men on the ground, scrap iron in front of them and a few rusty hammers, travelling blacksmiths, very low caste. Something was happening to the cows too. One of them chewed a torn plastic bag with some leftover food sticking to it as we waited for it to pass. These images choked me on the bouncy back seat, the same ones whose incomprehensible beauty I hadn't been able to take my eyes off yesterday. With a slight spin of the world, a slightly different angle of light, the same beings and things suddenly took on the twisted masks of death.

And just as rising nausea can be repeatedly caused and aggravated by a particular dish, a smell, a word that causes revulsion, even a colour, the bloodshot sight of those eyes now fanned my fever. It rose and would carry on rising as long as I saw those eyes in front of me. I tried, with all the force of reason I could muster, to press it back into the void from which it had so unexpectedly emerged. When this didn't work, I tried to turn my mind to something cool. Ice. To something technical – the needle of the jeep's speedometer. It was no use. The jeep lurched in and out of the ruts in the track, the needle danced wildly back and forth, offered me nothing I could cling onto, like the journey itself, whose meaning I no longer understood. Where were we going?

The professor kept trying to cheer me up. He turned round in the front seat to encourage me to hold out as the heat of the day reached its zenith. He knew of a house for me, I'd find healing and peace there, and as he said this he waggled his bald head in a manner that was hard to imitate, that dance of an Indian's head that could mean everything and nothing, smiling uncertainly, swaying back and forth between yes and no. I propped myself up and nodded. Good, good. As long as this is over soon.

The others urged me to go to a hospital, that was where I ought to be, but I was not to be moved. I wanted quiet, nothing more. Quiet and a few bottles of water. The professor kept out of the argument. When he saw that I wouldn't change my mind, he returned to his earlier proposal – 'an old hospital in an overgrown park'.

'A hospital? I'm not going to a hospital.'

He waggled his little head. 'One you'll like, a hospital with no doctors. It has been empty for a long time.'

'What did it use to be?'

'A home for lepers. It was abandoned when the new clinic opened.'

'Is it beautiful?'

'Amazingly beautiful. You'll find there what you need right now. Peace. Quiet. A good place. Of course, we'll leave you with everything you need.'

For a moment I felt slight distrust at how enthusiastically he was pressing the abandoned hospital upon me, but the thought of finally having some peace, no jeep, no noise, dispersed all my reservations. I accepted.

My friends gave up their resistance, and the professor began to talk. Once more I felt as if he were trying to placate us, but his stories were the only help now. It couldn't be much longer, he assured me; he knew every detail of the quiet, white hospital, founded by the maharaja, the old one, he stressed. The maharaja – I had seen his palace, we had driven along beside a never-ending wall, the tops of palm trees visible behind it, fancifully shaped towers and domes, a blend of every kind of occidental and oriental fairytale.

The professor told some stories about the maharaja.

He had always been a supporter of the new era, this was how he had introduced himself on the first evening in Jodhpur as our Indian guide and interpreter for this trip. And he had grown old with the new era. But somewhere along the way he had lost his progressive attitude, a little more with every passing day. He was overtaken by a defiant, grouchy desire to split open the ground he had spent his whole life stamping flat with his set, progressive views. A small, wiry man from a high caste, he would descend into grouchy laughter whenever he had to billet us in one of the many socialist guesthouses that still existed, all of which he appeared to know, where it was difficult to arrange for even the simplest of comforts and the once lavishly designed hostels looked so inhospitable and their rooms had the mildewed and airless feel of former party leaders having died in them.

I almost had to force him to tell me a maharaja tale that he considered unflattering, so fulsome was the former socialist's praise for these princes who had been chased from their thrones. Oh, that story about the dog-crazy maharaja of J. – it had been exaggerated abroad. The prince loved his dogs, yes, sure, and there had indeed been many of them, a great many even, but in his – the professor's – opinion, not 800 as was always claimed. More like 600 or perhaps only 400, it was easy to get it wrong, and it was well known that Europeans tended to exaggerate and endlessly embellish their Indian adventures. Incidentally, he doubted that each of these supposed 800 dogs had its own room and its own servants, as was rumoured. Quite a few Indian princes back then had been crazy about dogs, an English fashion from Queen Victoria's time. I wasn't willing to back down so quickly, I had read about this and was relatively sure of my facts, but he played everything down and diminished all the Indian excesses until hardly anything was left. 'An English fashion,' he repeated, 'Victorian decadence.'

I asked him about the dog marriages, wedding parties for the prince's favourite dogs celebrated by the whole court and lasting for days on end. Once more his dancing little head coiled away as if he were searching for a way out. Yes, that type of thing did occur, he confessed to my astonishment, but the maharaja whose lands we were now driving through had a special reason for this, a profoundly moving human story. Once, he was out hunting and as he was getting down from his elephant to take a closer look at the tiger he had shot, it attacked him and he was only saved by the fearless intervention of his hunting dogs, who were said to have thrown themselves at the merely wounded tiger, entirely against their nature, and saved their master from certain death. What appeared to foreigners like Indian folly was the prince's lifelong gratitude to the dogs, to all of them, irrespective of the individual animal and its merits.

Unfortunately, the professor remarked after a pause, the young maharaja was not like the old one, to the great regret of his maharani, a very sensible mistress, who was struggling to preserve what could be preserved of the previously powerful royal house's influence. The current maharaja showed not the slightest interest in this, however. 'Only sitar, sitar, day in, day out. And on major holidays, he plays to his monkeys, you have seen that for yourself.'

As he lamented the princedom's fate, the professor's

head rocked back and forth more and more violently. The jeep shook me about. Sweat ran down, warm as blood; my limbs ached; there was a pounding behind my forehead. The headwind brought no relief as it was boiling hot – it merely blew more heat at me – but I had to smile at the thought of the sitar-playing prince. The professor had surprised me. He had managed to obtain an invitation from the maharaja for us, he probably used his old caste connections for things like this. It was amazing to see that it all came so naturally to him. 'Not too hasty, not too leisurely,' he whispered to me as we walked towards the palace, and he wore his delighted smile the whole way, as if all eyes in the palace were upon us, which perhaps they were.

A servant was waiting for us at the gateway to lead us through dark corridors to a hall where we might recover from the journey. It was a hall of mirrors, not formal and solemn, just a folly. Hundreds or even thousands of tiny mirrors arranged in mosaics caught the red evening light that came in through the long, windowed façade, broke it up into umpteen thousand splinters and scattered them around the hall, which was filled with their twinkling. The servant brought refreshments and hot, damp towels like on an aeroplane and, who knows, maybe this custom had been brought to this palace from Business Class.

There was no hurry for things to take their course, there seemed to be ample time and we were left on our own. My awkwardness subsided when I saw how easily the professor took to the customs of the palace, how familiar this all was to him. He entertained us with tales from the prince's family history while we ate dried, bitter, red berries and Persian honey confectionery, and drank *lassis*. Just as the professor came to the ancestor who had restored puritanism, power and expansion to the state after a period of decadence and decline, the door was flung open and the prince entered. He bowed, asked after our health and invited us to a concert just before sundown on the west terrace, not waiting for an answer. Then the door was flung open again, and he was gone.

I could not even have said what he looked like, so quickly had all of this taken place. I was tormented by the idea of running into him around the palace and not recognizing him. As the sun set, the servant – he had stood as motionless as a sentry nearby the entire time – opened a double door and we followed him into a larger, more splendid hall, obviously the palace audience room. The chairs and divans were covered with brightly coloured blankets. The evening breeze was blowing in and drew a soft, high tinkling sound from the huge chandeliers as if they were silver-leafed treetops. This illusion was reinforced by the fact that the lamps themselves remained unlit and the audience room was in semi-darkness. Chairs were arranged in rows, with a larger chair on a dais, towards which the others were pointing. Life-size tiger claws stuck out from underneath the negligently draped sheet – the feet of the throne. Subjects had placed ritual gifts in front of it in the hope that the maharaja would look kindly upon them.

Now the tinkling of the chandeliers grew louder – a draught, the door to the west terrace was flung open. He sat dressed in white on a white cushion in all his turban-wrapped, sapphire-glinting maharaja finery, raised above the many subjects that attended and crowded about him. And his subjects were monkeys, nimble creatures with yellow-brown fur, scarcely bigger than rabbits. Many were still to settle down for good, quite a few were picking lice off each other, some had climbed up the side of the prince's podium, the most presumptuous were pulling at his cushion; the majority though were thronging and milling around him. My eyesight wasn't good enough to see everything there was to see, a thoroughly unnatural scene. The prince stood up, carefully set down his instrument, bowed to it, scattered rose petals and grains of rice in all directions, causing slight unrest among the monkeys, which subsided when he gave another quick, bouncy bow, picked up the large instrument again and sank back onto his cushion. That same instant, the first notes rose up.

Later, when everyone was bewitched, when the slowly, incredibly slowly fading light glowed on faces and even the professor – it was only now I understood what a highly volatile disposition he had – was overcome by the moment; he leaned over and whispered, 'The Bhimapalasi raga is so powerful it can even make animals cry.' The monkeys weren't crying now anyway. But they were sitting there quietly, completely out of keeping with their nature; that was miraculous enough. What did they hear? Did they hear what we heard, or just a strangely hypnotic sound that had cast a spell over them? At this moment, the monkey sitting closest to the prince was bold enough to stretch out its hand. I had watched it creep up timidly, carefully, as if approaching a fire – now finally the monkey's dark, hairy fingers stretched out towards the sitar lying in the lap of its player, and now it touched it, now it plucked one of the strings.

This image was my final memory of the evening. The heat had returned, the heat inside me and the heat we were driving through. I heard myself arguing with the professor. Actually, it was an argument with himself. As long as I kept mocking the princes, he defended them. However, as soon as the white man had a good word to say for the maharaja, the professor behaved like a progressive and ran him down. Might not the monkey prince, I asked him, be more in tune with the spirit of his ancestors than his progressive and power-hungry maharani, who adapted to modern times to save some scraps of what had been lost? He grumbled even more than before, then looked at me contemptuously.

'You,' he hissed, 'you want your Indian dream, your sitar dream with the monkey-loving rajas and rubies and diamonds as big as pigeon eggs on their turbans. That's true isn't it, that's what you want?' Then a crafty expression flickered across his face, and the jeep turned into the driveway before finally coming to a halt. 'Here we are,' he said.

We beeped the horn and waited for a sign of life that never came. Nobody else was here, we were alone. The abandoned hospital was a white, two-storey building, its two wings framing a courtyard. For a moment everything remained deathly quiet, then in the banyan trees the parrots raised a clamour at the intruders. As they shrieked excitedly, my companions fetched me out of the back seat of the jeep and led me up a wooden staircase to a circular gallery with many identical doors leading off it. Many of them were open, and I saw that the rooms were indeed empty, all of them.

The professor took the lead. He inspected every room and chose one for me. I took another look round from the gallery. What mighty trees the banyans were, their aerial roots as thick as an elephant's trunk. Small yellow monkeys were swinging around in them.

After some searching, a rickety chair was found, a small table in another room. The professor had chosen a room in which there was still a *charpoy*, the Indian day-and-night bedstead. The frame wobbled, it reacted to the slightest movement with a groan of its crooked, elaborately twisted legs. My friends carried in a foot-stool and a lamp from other rooms, they even brought a musty quilt and laid it over me. *Charpoy, charpoy*, object of humility, stretcher for the living, bed for the dead.

Then they stood there as if they were hesitating about leaving and wished they had already crossed the threshold. I wished so too. It's stuffy, they said, and they pulled the door and the windows open even wider, although they were already open and had been for years presumably, as a healthy person quickly says or does something practical before going out into the world leaving the sick man behind on his bed. At last they left. I saw their silhouettes in the doorway, heard their hurried footsteps down the stairs, heard the jeep start up and drive off and the renewed clamour in the banyan fall silent again. I was alone. The monkeys and the parrots had stopped screeching.

Sometimes, when I woke up for a few minutes, my hands on my musty sheets looking for a cool patch, I read things in the whitewash above me. In the world map on the ceiling. The monsoons of many summers had left their mark, the peeling paint gave it an aura of antiquity. Unexplored islands and continents could be seen, and the brownish watermarks represented contours and coasts. Occasionally, I was visited by images from the journey here.

⌒

Once, we had reached a remarkably tidy town and soon a wall with a high, wooden gate in it. Behind it lay a temple complex, itself the size of a town. The professor had directed our conversation to this ashram over and over again – yes, I had a feeling he had deliberately urged the driver to make a detour; now he preceded us through the gate, and we got out and followed him into the temple city.

Evenings on the road are special, places reached after days in the dust and the heat, the anticipation of gratification yet to be granted. That evening was pregnant with the afterglow of the day, the light on the marble temples and steps and sandstone squares had taken on the colour of wood anemones. Everyone was heading to the *puja* ceremony. I wanted to be alone, said to the others 'See you back at the jeep!' and disappeared around the next corner. My first impression remained. This town had none of the anarchy of Indian towns with their intense spiciness and sweetness, their absolute physicality and pervasive dampness. No betel spit, no beggars showing off their bodily defects in dramatic poses. No children, who immediately surround a stranger and start massaging his legs quickly and roughly, breaking off to make equally quick and rough eating signs. Grab leg, rub tummy, grab food. Leg, tummy, mouth, leg, tummy, mouth. No karmic succession of carts, burdens, destinies. Here, the wheel stood forever still.

I came to a large pilgrim hostel, or rather a pilgrim palace, and went inside. Adjusting to the half-darkness, I made out a high-ceilinged passageway, almost a hall. In alcoves along the sides, pilgrims were making themselves comfortable for the night, very simply. A mat to sleep on, a chair or a stool for the few things they carried with them. A grey-haired man smiled at me, a handsome, slender man with light-coloured eyes without a hint of blood or fever in them. It was easy to tell from the awkwardness with which he carried out these simple evening tasks that he was an academic. I spoke to him. Yes, he nodded, he had been a professor at a university and now he was old and on a pilgrimage. Had I come as a pilgrim too? My evasive answer encouraged him to keep talking, he was more absorbed in himself than by the exotic white man in this holy place anyway. He was considering leaving everything behind after a life of worry about his family, money and success, to devote the rest of his days to yoga and working on his karma. 'Clean your mind,' he said, 'like you clean your face before you go to sleep.'

I saw him lying on a pyre of stacked Arolia pine

somewhere on the banks of the icy mountain torrent beside which he had spent the final years of his life. The wind blew in and the river carried off his gently swirling ashes, which would mingle, weeks later, into the ocean. His face on his deathbed would wear the same slightly sceptical smile as it did now as he described his pious plans to me. At this moment, I felt a hand on my shoulder. A priest was standing next to me; I hadn't seen him coming, but he had obviously followed me.

'Come,' he said, and we went.

We went, and he paid no attention to the old man and pilgrim to whom I had been talking.

'Come.'

He wanted to show me something, the priest said, as I must be interested in yoga. He had ancient yogic texts in his cell, which I would normally never get to see. He took great strides, a small, slightly stocky man, his black beard standing out against the white of his robes. My attempts to make conversation about the temples we passed, their style and the like, were a failure. He wasn't listening. Now he stopped, told me to walk a few steps in front of him, and when I turned round, I saw that he was studying me scornfully. Had I already had dinner? When I said no, there was a triumphant flicker in his eyes, which contained none of the amazement of people in the villages. He didn't view me as an attraction, although that is exactly what I was – a white man who had walked straight into his arms. He looked at me as a cattle-breeder looks at his calf. He was not completely satisfied with what was in front of him. He was determined to act. However I declined his insistent urgings to accompany him to the refectory despite the fact that they would, he stressed, prepare a good meal for me there.

'See that beautiful light,' I said, and got ready to continue my walk through the temple town. He didn't spare a glance at the rose-tinted light.

'I show you light,' he said.

I was starting to feel like I should give him a try.

We walked past the great temple; it was unquestionably the focus of the sacred precinct as many pilgrims were climbing up its broad, steep, open steps. I wanted to follow them, but a look from the priest said: My friend, we have no time for that now, maybe later. He drew me on and I let him. It would be a while before the *puja* began, people were dawdling. He hurried ahead, ever deeper into the temple town, finally across one last square, through a door, up some stairs. There were some long tables. He had lured me into the refectory after all. I sat down with a shrug. A young priest-cook immediately appeared. My kidnapper made no fuss, he ordered for me and the boy soon returned with a tray full of steaming bowls, which he set down in a row in front of me. Vegetarian, as far as I could see.

I made a gesture of invitation, but the priest remained standing, suddenly a little self-conscious it seemed to me. I realized. Oh, how stupid of me to ask him to sit down at the table, unclean as I was. He couldn't eat with me, he wasn't even allowed to sit with me. He stood there, encouraged me to tuck in and watched me eat like a mother watching her returning, half-starved son. He kept pointing insistently to one particular bowl: 'Eat ghee!' He pushed the little bowl the size of a Chinese tea-cup, brimming with shiny yellow liquid butter fat, towards me. 'Eat all!'

To get it over with, I poured ghee over the okra vegetables I was eating at the time, almost all the fatty golden mass of ghee, kneaded one little ball after the other with my eating hand, dunked it in the ghee, wiped up the rest of the ghee while streams of ghee ran down my fingers, down my arm, over my mouth and chin and neck. I let it run and drip, leaned further forwards, wiped some more up and gulped it down, and when I had finished, I rushed out of the refectory, down the stairs – I couldn't bear the sight of another drop of ghee, let alone the smell. He came after me, his face glistening with joy, mine with ghee. He called, 'Look how energetic he walks now!', followed me across the square, which already lay in shadow, and guided me to his cell, which was close by. It was small, and I sank onto the stone floor; he fetched out the ancient texts as promised and sat down next to me. Calm settled upon our young friendship.

It was the start of a quiet hour during which he gave me tips about how to cleanse body and mind. I made a mental note of some of it, things like rinsing one's nose in the morning or that yoga initially violently arouses a beginner's sex drive, then it finally subsides after a certain amount of practice – but I have forgotten most of it. I asked whatever questions came to mind and he would occasionally open his treasure chest an inch to set me wondering about all I would stand to gain if I stayed here as his pupil. For that was what he wanted. When we reached this point, he made no bones about it. He put it to me directly and meant every word of it. He had found me, now he wanted to keep me. Stay with him, study for a long time, go the yogic way.

What was he thinking? Had the sight of this white man wandering around the temples awoken an ambition in him to pick someone for himself, to imitate his fellow countrymen who had become famous and sometimes rich because they had managed to win over large numbers of followers in the distant West suffering from wanderlust? Or was I being unfair to him, had he simply seen something he found irresistible in me? Either way, it would not be easy to get out of here, but he kept on courting me. I still had some questions to ask. When I asked him to tell me about certain practices that went further than one's physical and spiritual health, he smiled, but his smile froze into a polite mask.

'Oh yes,' he said, 'we can achieve a great deal.'

Tiredness began to dim his zeal. I could feel that he was giving up on me. He had scattered gold dust for me on the stone floor of his cell, and I was asking him for something better. For secrets that one was usually presented with at the end of the path. I didn't want the path, I wanted the secrets, right now, and I wanted to see them. I was just curious, he had misjudged me. I had asked questions like an antiques collector, I had wanted to tease things out that were not my due. I got up. He remained seated. As I left, he called something after me.

Night was falling, only the topmost roofs were still in the light. I found my way back to the temple easily. The rites had already begun, I was the last to skip up the marble steps. These not-yet-old, not-yet-worn steps, indeed the whole modern cleanliness of the town, everything indicated that these buildings dated from the Hindu reformation, which sought to renew and regenerate a religion that had grown weak under the Islamic Mughal emperors.

I reached the temple just as the gods appeared.

The crowd stood in dense-packed expectation. Bells were struck, cries of adoration rang out from all sides. At first, it was an effect of the light: the gods, having a second earlier been in their dark shrine, were suddenly illuminated. There were three of them. Three man-sized dolls. Several priests moved towards them – powerfully built men with bare chests – to dress them for *puja*. Sacrificial offerings were brought, the crowd's excitement swelled. Now, whether on a sign from the priest or not, everyone prostrated themselves before the gods. Another slight escalation and I would be the only one left standing. An impossible position. A sole static, stubborn stalk as the wind bends the pliant grass. This was not the time for such observations. This was a temple. These were gods. A movement was spreading that would not tolerate any refusal to move or at least made it look out of place. Join in or go. It was too late for that. A man called out something to me and when I didn't react, he pushed his way closer and repeated it. I still didn't understand him, but his gesture was unmistakable: Down! He could see that I was a stranger here and did not know the names of the gods nor the words of adoration that were now being moaned and shouted, louder and louder – but I could still show my devotion by throwing myself onto the stones in front of the gods like everyone else in the temple. He nodded to me in exhortation, not at all unfriendly; he wanted to help me and half-showed me how, come on, stranger, it's not hard. I stood there, stiff as a poker. It wasn't possible. Kneel before those three? Yes, kneel, it was a temple, those three were gods, not white marble statues in a museum. Quite some gods! Brightly adorned, garishly painted and cloaked in smoke, called to life by the priests who served them. Another wave of adoration ran through the temple like a strong wind, bending backs and heads, men and women; only the stranger stood. It is not possible, it is unnatural – prostrate oneself in front of them? Gaudy tricks, cheap dolls. It is very easy – what doesn't bend, breaks. Why not sink down at last, be one, forget your obstinacy? The man next to me, lying on the stones himself, took my hand, not roughly, quite gently in fact, and invited me to show the gods my love at last, 'a little, Mister, just a little'. Voices and bells, high-pitched and hoarse cries.

This couldn't go on. This couldn't go on any longer, not one second longer. I saw myself drop to my knees. I felt the soft, warm stone under my hands, then against my forehead. Above me there was an explosion of rejoicing.

〜

The first thing I felt when I woke up was an agreeable coolness. The heat of the day had passed, a light breeze blew through the room, the door swung on its hinges, the noise of the monkeys and parrots had ceased. I opened my eyes.

The gecko was sitting directly above me on the world map; he stuck there like a child's plastic dragon, utterly motionless, an extraordinarily fat specimen. Then I saw them all. They were lurking on the walls, in the corners of the room. They didn't move the whole time I was watching them – they crept out while I was asleep. As if they had more ancient rights, as if I were upsetting the order of the gecko world. Don't fall asleep now. In my sleep, I was sure, they secreted substances, drops on thin threads of mucus, which slowly sent me into a daze.

At one point I woke with a start. Perhaps a monkey out on the veranda. I bumped into something and struck a light – the malaria snake, the familiar sickly green slow-burning coil, a feature of every cheap room in the past weeks. My companions had left me one and urged me to light it. I hadn't done so. It glows throughout the night and spreads its disgusting fumes, which are said to keep mosquitoes at bay but which I knew poisoned my dreams. 'I will come to you in your dreams!' the yoga priest had called after me as I was leaving. 'You will see me again in your dreams.'

Thirsty, I was very thirsty. I found the water bottle, drank and poured the rest over me, all over me. A shiver ran through my body. Colours exploded on the inside of my closed eyelids, vermillion, saffron, scarlet, the red in the white of one's eye. It's just the heat, I told myself, the cursed Indian summer heat. More blue, I heard myself say. And it turned blue, the sumptuous final blue of the sky above dark trees before nightfall.

The Cricketer

I was waiting for the call. If it came, I would confirm the meeting, hang up, dial Omar's number. He would pick me up in his car, drive south along the desert road and drop me at the port of Ras al-Khaimah. A man would be waiting there to bring me out into the Gulf by boat, where the ship that would take me on board and to Singapore would be lying at anchor. But there was a little while to go until then.

I felt no desire to go out. Dubai is not a city you go out in, even when the temperature for once drops below 40 °C, which wasn't the case that month. It was the hottest time of the year, you went from one air-conditioned place to the next. There was even an ice rink, but I never saw anyone go ice-skating in the desert. No, no one in his right mind would go out for a walk here. What's more, the hotel in which I was waiting for the call was far too nice to leave. Go out on the terrace, swim a few lengths, doze. Order a tea with mint, and water with ice, lots and lots of ice, watch the Three Kings in the lobby, three young Arabs in ankle-length galabiyas and turbans in extravagant fairytale colours – royal blue, caramel, gold – as they sat there on the couch, holding hands, stroking feet, chatting. Or else I'd watch the doormen, two Sikhs. Their only job was to pull open the door of guests' limousines as they drove up and then the door of the hotel lobby while presenting their sabres. When the English lady pianist's time came, a small, never-changing, not very attentive audience assembled in the lobby and pre-tended to listen to the pieces by Chopin and Mahler she played sitting bolt upright.

᠆

The ship I was waiting for was an oil tanker, at the time one of the largest travelling the world's oceans and certainly the youngest in that summer in the nineties. I had been commissioned to describe this mode of transport and had phoned around until a shipping company agreed to take me on board one of their tankers. It was to take 2 million barrels of crude oil on its maiden voyage from Arabia to Singapore. It would stop on the open sea just for me, shortly before the Strait of Hormuz. It had a braking distance of many kilometres I had been told and it was impressed upon me to be scrupulously punctual for the meeting in Ras al-Khaimah. I shouldn't go thinking that the captain of an oil tanker could do whatever he liked, indeed he had to keep strictly to appointments, otherwise precious time would be lost, which could cause the shipping company great losses.

The call came after midnight. I dialled Omar's number, and he soon showed up. We drove along the lighted desert road towards the Sultanate of Oman in silence. We were the only ones on the road that night, other than occasional semi-wild camels that crossed the immaculately smooth road provocatively slowly, paying no regard to Omar's flashing lights and curses. At some stage, we turned off for Ras al-Khaimah and got out. I couldn't see my hand in front of my face. It wasn't darkness Omar left me in, it was pitch-blackness. No stars, no lights, not a single distress signal, just impenetrable night and the wall I leant against while waiting for the man with the boat.

He was on time. I heard him when he stood directly before me and walked in front of me, then the soft slapping of the waves covered his shuffling steps. He helped me into the open boat, started the engine and headed out at speed. The Persian Gulf lay there like a forest lake on a moonless summer's night, silent and black. And hot and humid, to remind us that we were in Arabia. I sat on the thwart and lost all sensation of where I was, where the sea ended and the sky began.

At some point, a signal appeared, uncertain at first, then a clear red. I couldn't say how close or far away it was, the complete darkness didn't permit that. Yet the signal grew, the red burned more fiercely. A fresh, jagged weld in the sky. I stared at it until I realized: the jagged line was a ridge, those were mountains, and the red was the sun rising behind the mountains of Oman. There was nothing rose-fingered, nothing Franciscan about this sunrise. Arabia's sun was not the friendly sun of our songs. It was naked, red-hot violence. Now the flaming ball shot up angrily, the terror of the world. In minutes it had asserted its despotism – everything bowed its head and covered itself.

I only noticed the tanker when the boatman dropped his speed and heaved to. I threw my head back – the cliff before us was it. Rearing up vertically, it blocked out most of the sky and the sea. There was nothing ship-like about it, just this gigantic wall above me. They had lowered some steps, which dangled down from the monster as delicately as a cobweb. I started to climb up the swaying, endlessly long, light metal ladder, one hand on the railing, suitcase in the other. From time to time, the pinhead of a sailor appeared high above me to see how far the insect on the steel hull of the ship still had to go. Shortly before I reached the top, I turned round and watched the boat as it sped home towards Ras al-Khaimah, until it was no more than a vague dot on the water.

I was led to the guest cabin and immediately afterwards to the captain, a man of calm authority whose commands one would instinctively obey in an emergency. He briefly explained the route and the main onboard routines to me and invited me to have a drink with him in the bar that 'evening'. This was an expression from back home as it turned out, for what we call evening did not exist here. Night fell as we passed Hormuz and headed out into the Arabian Sea. It was always night that fell, never evening.

⌣

On the first day I had eyes only for the sea in its boundless – and for the ship in its mechanical – splendour. The ship's inhabitants' radius was small. Just as there are countries that are largely desolate and empty and only inhabitable along small coastal strips, so it was with the oil tanker. The deck was an ever-hot, life-destroying landscape, painted green as if out of spite and made up of vents, marked paths, measuring instruments whose purpose I didn't understand, and other mysterious structures. Above all, however, there were pipes: fat ones, thin ones, ones that ran along the ground and others on props, as well as the lattice steps leading up and over them. The largest bundle of pipes ran over head height from the bow to in front of the bridge, dividing it into equal-sized left- and right-hand fields. As far as possible, people avoided spending time out here. It was no place for humans, so unbearable was the blazing sun.

The ship's residents lived in the superstructure that, well, towered over the deck, but that word isn't quite right. It sounds too much like castle or castle forecourt and there was no such harmony here. From up on the bridge, the topmost part of the superstructure, one could always watch one or two unlucky fellows going about their business on the deck under the despotic sun. From the very first day, the sea ate away at the new ship and so sailors were sent out with pots of paint and paintbrushes to keep the rust at bay. They were not talkative, they wanted to get it over with quickly and they looked like prisoners under guard. And indeed they were, for the bridge saw everything.

However, I had seen enough of the green paint and grey waves of the outside world and I retreated into the inhabited part of the ship. Not many people lived in the superstructure – a dozen officers and barely more sailors – and I quickly became familiar with them. Yet this was not only down to their number. There was something tricky about our shared situation, something that made us act cautiously and discreetly, at least that's how I perceived it. We were the flea in the giant's ear. All of us worked with a steady hand to keep him happy and up to speed, anything to avoid braking, anything to avoid deviating from our course. It was as if we were riding a Mesozoic beast, vastly superior to us, its drivers, in both power and mass, and capable at any moment of shaking us off with one angry buck and destroying us. A giant that, for the moment, let itself be steered so it ploughed through the Indian Ocean at 15 knots.

The steel-mantled sea of oil we were travelling on was enough to blow up a city. The seamen knew that, but they never thought about it. They thought about appointments, maintenance work, the checks they had to make. They stuck to technical jargon, even when they were chatting and smoking a cigarette. I never saw any of them run or even talk hurriedly. They were tanker drivers even on land – I was to witness this – and presumably in their sleep too. They had a very physical awareness of their whale-like ship, whose slightest movement had tremendous consequences.

I didn't see a drop of oil, but I smelt it day and night. It was in the officers' mess and in my cabin, it was on the bridge and in the corridors. It was on your skin in the morning when you washed and on your palate when you brushed your teeth, it was on your bed-sheets in the evening. Nothing and no one was free of the smell of oil. No one spoke about it, it was just one of those things that are as they are, and did not need to be spoken of. And this was how everything seemed on board: orderly. Who, where, when, had to do his duty. How many drinks were allowed with the captain or without him of an evening. Who had to greet whom and who give orders to whom.

There were two nations and two classes. The officers, who also included the engineers, were each and every one of them English; the crew came from the

Philippines to a man. The officers took their three meals a day in the officers' mess, the sailors at the large crew table in the crew's quarters. And there were two times on board – free time and work time. And there was St John, the Second Officer.

I had first seen him on some outside steps as I was climbing up and he was coming down backwards. For a moment I had thought he too was a guest on board, whose presence had been kept secret from me. But he was the Second Officer, and there was a reason for his unsailorlike behaviour. He was practising going down stairs backwards. He was constantly practising, but mostly cricket. Whenever he got the chance, he would fiddle around with his cricket bat. Whether he was having a conversation or wandering up and down on the bridge at night. These air-shots, shots without the ball, accompanied only by the whistle of willow, had become synonymous with him. If you saw their shadow or reflection on a wall or in a window, you saw him. There were therefore multiple versions of him on board. He roamed about. He had heard or sensed me on the steps at the last moment.

'Who goes there?'

'A passenger.'

He turned round and quickly sized me up. His eyes were grey, sea-grey. 'So you're the one. Let's have a drink some time!'

St John, that's what everyone called him. I never found out whether this was his surname or a nickname; I never asked because the name immediately struck me as suiting him. A member of the wandering brotherhood. He was young, not yet 30, and he didn't behave like the other officers. Their hair was short and their caps and officers' jackets straight; his hair was shoulder-length, stringy, and he wore his white uniform like a cigarette butt in the corner of the mouth, a bit lop-sided. They gave you a friendly greeting when you crossed paths; he would have barely noticed me if he hadn't stumbled upon me. No, he wasn't like the others, not as factual as them; he was something straight out of a sailor's song.

Neither of those was with us anymore, not the songs nor the men who featured in them; I knew that from travelling on this tanker. Here were hard-working specialists and a box full of videos. The person on watch on the bridge steered the ship. The duty engineer climbed down into the huge engine room and worked in a temperature of 70 ºC. And anyone who was off duty watched videos. *Bad Lieutenant* was popular at the time. The cassettes were replaced in every large port by a new box of videos, just as fresh vegetables used to be brought on board to prevent scurvy in earlier times. And there was the satellite telephone. The officers used it to ring home. St John never sat in front of the television and never rang home.

That night, reluctant to go to sleep without having seen the stars of Arabia, I went up onto the bridge. When you stand beneath a clear sky on a summer's night far from large cities, it is as if a veil has been drawn back. The moment I reached the bridge, I raised my eyes and saw a velvet canopy embroidered all over with diamonds. So bright, so sparkling, so shockingly close.

'Impressed?'

St John was standing beside me. I nodded.

'First time?'

I nodded again. He casually raised two fingers to his cap in greeting and said that he'd take another look at the baby. I saw him check the radar screen and the course set by the autopilot through the glass. He motioned to me that I was welcome to come inside, but I stayed where I was. The air was warm and humid as it was during the day and much more pleasant; the great despot was busy burning the other side of the earth. I wanted to drink my fill of the stars with my eyes but soon realized that this wasn't possible. I went inside.

He didn't seem to mind having a bit of company in his glass turret. The radio was turned up loud, a crackling and groaning out of which, now and again, guttural Arabic voices rolled in like waves from the distance. Some of what they said sounded technical and routine, as if they were giving coordinates or commands, but I got the impression there was also some chat. St John showed me the chart table on which he was constantly plotting our course, and explained the instruments to me. I asked about the green, insect-like symbols crawling over the radar screen.

'Echoes of other ships.'

'And their twitching antennae?'

'Their course.'

It was better to keep an eye on them, he mumbled. Ships were crossing our path all the time, but they didn't react to our radio messages. 'Ghost ships. Crew overtired or drunk; the captain's switched on the autopilot and gone to sleep.' He picked up his bat and unfurled a stroke. 'Not everybody out here is as straight and as sober as us.'

Then he spoke of the typhoons he had seen while travelling on container ships in the North Pacific. He put his bat away and used both arms to show how a typhoon grabs a ship. How it lifts it up and hurls it back into the canyons of sea-water. How it throws the seamen back and forth. 'Like dice being thrown!' He clung to the edges of the chart table as if it were just about to happen. Then he let go with a shrug of the shoulders. 'This here is nothing,' he said, pointing out into the Arabian night. 'This is for lovers.'

'How long have you been at sea?'

He picked up the bat again and examined the wood. 'Let's think – it must be ten years all told.'

'And when were you last on land?'

'On land ...' The bat swished through the air. 'They play cricket there. Do you know anything about cricket?'

'No, unfortunately.'

He nodded. 'Yes, it's an odd game. You're always running. You hit the ball and you run. And it takes up a lot of time; some games last for days. And a lot of space. Here, we've got the time, we just haven't got the space. Oh, I see you're tired. Pardon me for my carrying on like that. Sleep well.'

'When will someone come and relieve you?'

'Tomorrow morning. Goodnight.'

'Goodnight.'

I stayed outside for a few minutes longer. The stars were every bit as magnificent as before, but my eyes wandered. I saw the Second Officer in his cockpit: he was now totally absorbed in his cricket shots, surrounded by flickering green radar screens, and exhibited as if he had been shut into this feebly lit glass box for scientific observation.

That wasn't necessary. He obviously sought out

the night watch. He probably volunteered for it. The captain and his First and Second Officers shared the watch around the clock. The three of them steered the ship, through the Persian Gulf yesterday, through the Arabian Sea today, in the Indian Ocean tomorrow. Yet it was often the Second Officer I met on the bridge at night. I too grew to love these nights. They were the best thing the tanker had to offer. During the indigo hour at the bar with the captain, I stole glances at the clock and the following morning I slept in. My rhythm fell in with St John's rhythm.

The voices that came to us over the marine radio service changed. The Arabic stopped and we were now accompanied by the guttural languages of the Indian subcontinent. We headed towards Bombay, followed the west coast of India and set our course around the southern tip of Sri Lanka. Once more night had fallen, supper in the officers' mess was over and the captain's round of drinks that followed had been survived. I climbed up the ladder out into the open air. The stars had arrayed themselves as always, inconceivably bright and close. But what was that? I could scarcely believe my eyes. Tonight the ocean contrived to reflect the starry sky. In whichever direction I looked we were moving through a sea of glittering, moving lights. The world was transformed; so was the tanker, an airship gliding through a swarm of glow-worms. It was a perfect illusion, but it soon melted away: these were the lanterns of fishing boats off Sri Lanka's southern cape, one burning on every boat, a single one, and there were hundreds of boats. I leaned over the railing and watched some of those closest to us. Lights adrift on the open sea. Rocked about by the swell from the tanker, which – at least this was how it seemed on board – forged ahead with utter calm through the peaceful ocean. The pitch-black colossus cut its unerring path through the sea of lights. Had we ploughed a few boats under, we would not even have noticed. We could only stick to our course: the tanker's braking distance was several times longer than the Sri Lankan swarm was wide.

When I looked round, I saw him dancing. Holding the bat in both hands, he was taking slow, painfully precise steps that looked more like t'ai chi than a game of cricket. The door was open; Dravidian voices, crackling electrically, seeped out. Now was not the time to disturb him.

The images of that night were not to be repeated. We now moved across the open sea and the only thing to be seen from time to time was another merchant ship in the hazy distance. One day I spotted land. One of the Andaman Islands, the seamen said, puzzling over whether it might be the one on which lepers from Bengal used to be interned. The ship moved past all these islands, peninsulars, shorelines without once calling at them. The only thing the seamen knew about them was what was required for navigation purposes. They were truly men of the sea. Contacts with land were necessary, but they were kept as rare and as short as possible, if only due to the harbour fees. Load and unload and then off – to sea, to sea.

It was two nights since I had last met St John on the bridge. The night after we passed the Andamans, he was doing his rounds again, the door was open once more, there were now Malaysian sounds coming over the radio. We were approaching our destination

– Singapore. There, several sailors would disembark to see their homeland and their families again. They worked on the ship for months at a time, some even choosing not to go ashore at the few ports the tanker called at, sending all their wages home except for a little pocket money they kept for themselves. After spending some time with their wives and children in the Philippines, they would go back to sea again for months on end. The officers' tours of duty were shorter, they saw their homeland more often.

Tonight St John was neither walking back and forth, nor practising. His bat was leaning against the wall. I entered, greeted him and bent over the maritime chart, the first thing I had done each previous night, when he had been pleased to explain our route to me, or at least that was how it had felt to me. I followed the lines through the Strait of Malacca with my index finger and stopped off Singapore. Somewhere there, we could drop anchor outside the harbour and our cargo of oil would be unloaded at sea. The captain had told me this, and the officers and the men were now forming into groups of those who wanted to take a water taxi to

Singapore. I asked the Second Officer if he was going on land as well.

'Singapore.' He spoke it as if might jolt his memory. 'What would I do there?'

'As far as I know, they have cricket matches there.'

He made himself busy with the charts, calculating, drawing. While appearing to look at his results, he suddenly said, 'I've tried, you know.'

'You mean, on land?'

'Yes, on land.' He corrected a detail in his chart entry. 'I wanted to pack all of this in.' He threw the pencil his fingers had been playing with onto the chart table. 'There were parents there. There was a girl there who wanted to marry me, and I wanted her too. There was even a job, and not a bad one at that. Everything was set up nicely for me.'

'And?'

'Four months, then I couldn't stand it any longer. Driving to the office, coming home in the evening, barbecues with friends, going out with people from work, sitting in the living-room talking with friends, talking about insurance, there's so much talking – there.' He made a fluttering movement with his hand in the general direction.

'And now?'

'I'm back at sea. But not like before. I don't long for land anymore.'

He took his bat and checked how it felt in his hand. He tried to find a good position, legs well apart but not too wide, fixed his eyes on the imaginary ball, now he swept forwards, went through with the stroke and hit. Now he should have set off for a run towards the other end of the pitch. Green insects crawled across the screens, their antennae trembling. A Malaysian voice spoke, a woman's voice; not once on this journey had I heard a woman speak over the maritime radio. We didn't understand what she said, but her voice was soft and dark – the crackle of the radio couldn't hide that – and the glass control box in which we stood in the heat of the night was flooded with yearning. We hardly dared breathe. When the voice stopped, it was as if the needle had lifted off a well-loved record. Maybe it was just the crackling that gave me that impression. We didn't say another word. I left. It was our last conversation.

Next morning, the captain summoned the officers and the passengers. He made a short speech, in which he reminded us of the threat of a pirate attack, which could happen at any moment in the Strait of Malacca. The shipping company had placed advertizements in the major newspapers in the surrounding countries to point out that no cash was held on their ships. As ours was not a container ship, he thought it unlikely that we would be attacked, however tankers had been hijacked in the past and had disappeared without a trace along with their oil. Then the captain ordered us to wedge our doors shut so they couldn't be forced open from the outside. Naturally, as we gentlemen well knew, this was no guarantee, pirates were known to close in out of the radar's blind spot and board from the stern. His second instruction was therefore that anyone not on watch should lock himself in his cabin at night and not open the door, whatever happened.

After the daily roll call, we stood around together for a little longer. One of the engineers turned to me and said that the one man on board who had experienced an attack by pirates and just about survived it was not here, unfortunately. I had no trouble guessing whom he meant. 'That mad dog,' he continued and once more told the adventure all of them knew by heart. 'They came from astern, as always.' And to me, the landlubber guest: 'The stern is lower than the rest of the ship. It's easy to board there with a well-thrown anchor rope. It was night, the crew were asleep. The watch on the bridge was still doubled back then. St John and his former captain only noticed the pirates when they already had their machine-guns trained on them. They tied them both to their chairs, gathered up everything they could take, put the ship on autopilot and disappeared. The crew, safe in their cabins, hadn't noticed a thing. For hours the ship steered straight ahead, for hours St John and the captain tried to free themselves; at any moment they might ram into another ship, a reef or something else.' It all ended well though, for they managed to break free of their bonds and take control of the ship's wheel again.

We waited for nightfall with some trepidation.

That afternoon we had entered the Strait of Malacca and this also made things easier for the pirates, as every ship that passed through the channel had to radio the control centre that piloted all traffic through. Anyone eavesdropping on these radio communications could obtain precise information about the positions of interesting ships and could pick out one of those on offer for whose cargo he had a distribution network ready and waiting. The captain's round was a brief and silent affair that evening. I followed instructions and, instead of going up onto the bridge, locked my cabin door from the inside and soon fell asleep. When I woke up the following morning and opened the door, everything was as usual. No pirates had come.

⤳

We reached Singapore before sundown. Pilots came on board and manoeuvred the tanker to an unloading installation at sea, into the middle of a herd of other tankers. While the engineers set about pumping out the 2 million barrels of crude oil, water taxis were ordered for Singapore. Most of the seamen would come back by the same means a few hours or a night later; for me, now was the time to say my goodbyes. I had already bid the captain, the officers and the sailors farewell. Yet I was in no hurry. I seemed to be drawing things out. The last water taxi was waiting just for me, the others had already gone.

It was an open boat like the one that had waited for me in Ras al-Khaimah, but taxi was an exaggeration. During its long life, this boat had transported just about everything imaginable, both living and dead. An old, dark-brown, incredibly hunched Malay was crouching, his spindly legs tucked underneath him, on a bar stool in front of the tiller. He fiddled around, and the engine awoke from its slumbers with a rattle. I looked up one last time, it was the same view as that early morning in the Persian Gulf.

Above me, a familiar face appeared. No, St John wasn't going ashore. He was right: what would he do there? He belonged to the sea. I shouted up a greeting. He put his hand to his cap, which was askew as always. Then he slowly disappeared from sight.

The boat set its course for the city. It was a different world from the one in which I had boarded the ship. It was warm and humid here too, but it was softer – it had none of the hardness of the desert. There was nothing tyrannical about the sun here. It stood large and mellow above the water, wavering, as if drawing out the fading day for one final minute. It now rolled out a red, gently rippling carpet across the water, and fittingly this was the way to Singapore.

Mekong Mama

The morning I went on board was one of rain and red loam. The rain fell dense and silent and warm, like an inescapable fate. The path to the pier was long. When I got to the spot where the boat to Phnom Penh was supposed to cast off, the white suit I had been wearing since I arrived had been transformed into a wet, red-brown rag up to above the waist. The *Mekong Mama* was easy to find; it was the only boat that morning. It was small to have such an expansive name; it lay deep in the water, which reached up to just below the few, close-set little windows.

A narrow plank led on board, so slippery that even

the most cautious of steps made it rock unpredictably. The passengers tried to adjust, each after his own fashion, either by surrendering, bending their knees and rocking with it or else making an obvious decision to stiffen in order to quell the ludicrous swaying beneath their feet. Neither was successful. The plank outfoxed the supple because it would start to rock unexpectedly at a different frequency, upset their rhythm and force them into grotesque balancing acts. And it made those who sought to preserve their dignity stumble all the more, so that they flung themselves with flailing arms onto the safety of the deck, where the boatmen not infrequently had to catch them. The plank treated everyone alike, making all look equally ridiculous. Everyone had their work cut out to make it across.

With my suitcase in my left hand, I looked around for a makeweight for my right hand, saw the heavily laden man in front of me hesitate, offered to carry one of his boxes tied up with string, and ventured, with both arms outstretched, out onto the plank. It wasn't going to break – it was too springy for that – but the boat's crew seemed to be hanging about hoping one of us passengers would slip and fall into the water. The men watched us embark almost absentmindedly and yet nothing escaped their attention. I even thought I detected them willing someone to fall in, especially when that someone was one of their few white charges.

'Don't lift your feet! Keep them on the plank! Slide, Monsieur, slide!'

I recognized the voice behind me and did as it said. He was right, it was pointless resisting the rocking or deliberately trying to rock with it; it was impossible to control either way. I jumped onto the boat and turned round, the cardboard box in one hand and the small, battered metal suitcase, my faithful companion, in the other. The man who had spoken to me from behind jumped after me onto the deck, which was at the same time the roof of the boat, slightly convex and decorated more than delimited by a thin, ankle-high bar. It was just about strong enough to be able to push my feet against it lightly when the boat set off. The roof was not actually designed to carry passengers; they were likely to slip off at any moment if there were a bit of swell, but nobody seemed worried about that. The crew weren't bothered if you looked for a free space there. I hesitated.

'It is better to stay up on top, Monsieur.'

'What about the monsoon – six hours of storm and heat?'

'If the boat sinks, Monsieur, the people down below' – with the tip of his foot he tapped on the roof, beneath which the passengers were squashing themselves onto a few benches – 'have no chance. They won't get out fast enough and will drown, or else they'll just about get the door open but won't be able to swim away from the drag of the sinking boat.'

'And we jump off the roof in time and do the crawl towards the crocodiles?'

His expression didn't change. 'It's your choice, Monsieur.'

I had watched the crocodiles for an entire afternoon – there was a farm close to the temple ruins. No, not just crocodiles – a landscape of crocodiles, leathery and greeny-brown. Hundreds, thousands perhaps, motionless in their concrete pools. It all looked more geological than animal, as if they were not being kept there but rather observed, foreign matter growing extremely slowly. Inadvertently I lingered in front of this crocodile lava, watched it throbbing with a subterranean pulse and stirred by imperceptible breaths. One could make out aged dragons and specimens of every size, right down to the tiniest. Many jaws were wide open, their teeth reminiscent of salt-corroded groyne stumps at low tide. They lay as if under a spell, piled up immobile on top of each other in the milky afternoon light of Siem Reap. The name of the town meant '*Siam-de-fā*,' the hotel manager had explained to me in his Khmer French on the first evening, and when I didn't immediately understand, he made a victory sign. Victory over Siam. Siam défait. 'Khmer victoire!' he called, and then in German, 'Siam kaputt!'

A boy had come into the crocodile farm holding a squealing animal in his hand, bigger than a rat, smaller than a marten. He grabbed it by one of its hind legs, swung it around and then launched it into one of the pools. The petrified leather immediately broke up, and in a lithe feeding frenzy, which had been unthinkable

69

mere moments earlier, the crocodiles shot towards their prey; it was torn apart in seconds.

What was I doing here? I had come to Singapore by sea, had stayed one or two nights in the small Chinese-run hotel near the great Hindu temple, had walked through the days' sticky heat, had – because that is what you do there – stood in Raffles Hotel bar in the twilight and later, in the Indian quarter, had a fortune-teller in a blue sari read in my palm that I would have a happy journey that would end with a happy return home and a happy marriage with many happy children. After another confused, sticky day I had got into the long-distance bus for Thailand. It drove north up the peninsular through the Malaysian night and my only recollection is of a few stilt houses in the jungle caught in our headlights and the outdoor food stand whose rancid wares were so fly-spotted that I couldn't bring myself to eat anything even though I was very hungry.

In the grey morning light, the bus drove into southern Thailand; in the evening I lay on an island beach, Buddha Beach, and in a few minutes learned to ride a moped. I swam out to sea, took the moped for another spin, then got a lift back over to the mainland and took the night train to Bangkok, with a compartment to myself so I could lie undisturbed on the bed and keep a look-out for lights, how they appeared, slid past and disappeared. Beneath a naked light bulb in front of his hut, an old Malay absorbed in a lonely game; under a neon tube a young woman with her child in her arms, walking up and down a bare room, up and down. In the weak glimmer of their cigarettes, three or four men in a car, in their wrap-around skirts, smoking, saying nothing, smoking. The night was too magnetic for me to be able to sleep, with all the small epiphanies of this tropical journey. Then came the blackest hour when nothing more appears and everything crawls into itself. I wrapped myself in my thin sheet and fell into a thin sleep, waiting for the early light – it would wake me. When I awoke, it was bright, hot daylight. We were just drawing into Bangkok.

The watercolours had trailed away, the world in my window was increasingly taking on form and rhythm. Paddy fields, with the silhouettes of women planting in them, bending forward incessantly, diving in like cormorants fishing. Wherever there was a flash of gold, the morning sun was sparking a temple roof. That too trailed away. The gaps were decreasing fast, the world becoming more crowded, until it was crowded. The train rolled into the denser, higher-rising suburban piles of huts and houses, yards, workshops, sheds, mopeds, cars, chicken cages; all the fences and dwellings that contain wishes and hardships, before one day they simply disappear. One giant container site – that's what Bangkok looked like to me. An expressway on stilts ran directly past the windows of the hotel I had moved into. Although I hadn't been looking for it, I found the travellers' street immediately; it was like any other backpacker street. Night fell once more. I found the river that slides through the city, ate a strangely tasteless Thai dish and soon took the aeroplane into Cambodia.

⌒

The light aircraft banked over the ruins of Angkor before coming in to land. For as far as I could see, the plain was flooded; it reflected the dark-grey monsoon sky and occasionally, for a few seconds, us as well. Then a light metal insect flitted in over the water, just like some bugs that can walk on a pond or puddle, so light that the film of the water bears their weight. The airport lobby in Siem Reap was a small, rough building; a small, rough committee met us in silence, half a dozen soldiers or other uniformed people behind a table. My passport wandered from hand to hand; I followed it, not once letting it out of my sight. I didn't know whether they knew what they were supposed to do with the passport and the man who came with it. Whether at any moment something might happen, something loud and lashing, something hoarse that would blow away this pantomime of a dignified routine that didn't exist and commit us all to the insignificance to which we so obviously belonged.

The hotel was a single-storey, double-winged building arranged around a courtyard which had been built on the prospect of an imminent upsurge in tourism to Angkor Wat and the Bayon and the other ruins of the Khmer empire lying buried in the jungle, once the last mines had been cleared. A smiling young woman in close-fitting traditional costume was busy all day with her broom destroying self-renewing columns of ants as they worked their way across the veranda and into the kitchen and under the doors into the guest rooms, as well as providing the stone-grey Buddha statue with fresh red flowers. Every morning around seven, the door of the room next to mine would be pushed open and a burly Khmer would step outside. Wearing only a pair of trunks with a revolver stuck in them, he went down to the river to swim a few strokes, came back with water trickling down his taut skin and disappeared into his room, not to be seen again that day.

I spent most of the time before the heat of noon at the ruins, and most of the time when the heat abated in an armchair at the Grand Hôtel d'Angkor, often forgetting to write down sentences in my notebook, distracted by the peaceful sensations of those sultry afternoons. American and Chinese pioneer tourists, their colourful shirts, their regular habits. Little bubbles floating on a bowl of tea. Here now, then gone. The feeling of being there at a fragile moment that might burst at any time. Like the bomb that went off a few days later at Siem Reap aerodrome. The Grand Hôtel was all too bold a statement, its equanimity, its noiseless houseboys and gently whirring ventilators, its sparkling silver cutlery. I held my breath. The aftershocks of years of bloody rice fields reverberated on, their power remained; I could sense and sometimes see it, and it wasn't just the skulls gathered in the fields, piled up in the pagodas, it wasn't just the one-legged, the one-eyed, the agile hoppers along the mined paths. It was in the air. It was in the water, in the bread, in everything. It still lurked in the doorway, suddenly revealed itself in the mirror – briefly. For the noise of the coming times already filled the bars.

I sometimes went to one, the Red Piano, where the first returning whites sat. The blackness inside is my only specific memory – the bar's irregularly shimmering black walls. And him. That is where he first caught my eye. He came in late in the evening, sat down at a table by the window, ordered tea – nobody ordered tea here – and let it go cold. His head was shaved, he wore a threadbare but well-cut black suit and underneath it a black T-shirt with a small hole in the vicinity of the heart; it wasn't a joke or a bullet, it was just a hole. He had wound the checked cloth we know from war photos around his neck. The cloth and the sagging black of the suit gave him a Khmer Rouge look, there was something monk-like about his shaven head. I couldn't figure him out, I wasn't even sure whether he was white or Asian. Weren't there whites with a yellow-ish complexion, and didn't people who had lived here for a long time and not grown red-faced from the heat and vice over the years take on the same skin colour as the man over by the window? I had no reason to speak to him; he remained a stranger to me.

In the evening of a day I had spent among the ruins, dozing away the midday heat in the cool semi-darkness of a temple, I climbed a hill. At the top, I had been told, a crowd would gather at sunset to worship or just to enjoy the view. It was a moment lifted out of time. The broad plain in the haze of the low sun, the weath-ered spikes and godheads of the temples looming up out of the forest – a moment during which nothing else on earth existed or counted. For a while I thought

I could see what their builders might have seen when they stood up here. The view of kings. I was gripped by a longing to be here, here forever more. A desire for something lasting. For land. For days that end like this one, in this red light of kings. I looked around me. Scattered groups sat on carved stones or on the grass. Backpackers in their trekking uniforms. Young Khmers who had come up to be free for an evening. Monks in their red robes too. People laughed, passed a bottle around, let rosewood beads slip through their fingers and shared the stolen hour, pyramid-high above everything that had happened down there before, everything that was still to come.

I only saw him when he stood next to me. He spoke in French. 'Or would you prefer English? Unfortunately I do not speak German. Peaceful evening, isn't it?'

'A peaceful evening. How do you know who I am?'

'Practice. Don't worry, I'm not stalking you, I know nothing about you.'

He chatted for a while. He was wearing his black suit, I my white one. I wanted to get him to introduce himself, so I introduced myself. He gave a crooked smile and tapped his head. 'Forgive me – the usual courtesies, I sometimes forget them.' He gave a Khmer name. 'It was most impolite of me to disturb you here. May I invite you for a drink at the Red Piano later?' I accepted, and he walked away. He did not appear in the bar that evening.

I walked through the town and when I stopped in front of a pizzeria that was as temporary as anything else in a place after war, the things I had heard about it came back to me. You should have a bit of fun for once and order a Happy Pizza from the waiter: it was not on the menu but would be made to order. I went inside; the menu was lying on the table, a dog-eared sheet of paper, the Happy Pizza wasn't on it.

'A Happy Pizza, please,' I said when the waiter came.

'Happy Pizza, Monsieur?'

'If you don't mind.'

He looked at me, looked round with a grin, studied me again. 'Happy-happy Pizza?'

'Happy, cela suffit.'

'As you wish, Monsieur.'

He brought some water and, after a while, something that looked like the bare bits of yeast bread the size of a vinyl record single our village baker used to make when I was a child. I ate it.

Back at the hotel, the young woman in her Khmer dress was standing on my veranda topping up the glass of my stocky next-door neighbour, who was now dressed. Ice tinkled in his glass like Christmas chimes. He was playing with his revolver. Pushed his finger through the trigger guard, spun the weapon round on the table, let go, looked closely at which way the barrel was pointing, was satisfied with his oracle and consulted it again. It was only when the barrel was clearly pointing towards him that he stopped.

The television set in my room was showing the one and only programme. A man talked and talked. Followed by a different man about something else. Suddenly things got funny. A woman – was it Condoleezza Rice? – was visiting a nursery school – wasn't that North Korea? – and the children sang for her, then she sang for the children in karaoke style, everyone was dancing and singing and clapping their hands and looking happy. Including me. It had been so long since I'd last laughed like this. Bang! A shot. I tore the door open. My neighbour was standing there and laughing too; only the girl in the Khmer dress wasn't laughing. He had shot the Buddha straight through the forehead. I went over and touched the spot, the edge of the bullet hole was still warm and, even more surprisingly, a draught of cool air was streaming out of it, so welcome in the humid, mosquito-ridden night.

I fell asleep and dreamed of a column of ants, they were so big you could ride the ants and lead them by the reins. The caravan of giant ants was commanded by a woman who looked like Condoleezza Rice when she took off her Bedouin veil to retie it. And whenever we made a stop, which was seldom, there was a Happy Pizza – she took it out of her handbag and handed it to each of us after taking the first bite, the *jus primae pizzae* unquestionably hers. In all the long years I've been an ant-leader, I've never seen or even heard of anyone of us ever begrudging her this privilege or any protests about it, as was later rumoured. That is a pack of lies.

The morning after this night, I went to the boat still feeling a little happy; perhaps the waiter had misunderstood me and asked the kitchen for a 'Happy-happy' after all. I would find out if I ever came back.

～

Not long after the *Mekong Mama* had cast off, a rowing boat drew alongside. Boxes were thrown from hand to hand, and our low-riding boat sank deeper still. Then the engine screamed into life, we began to move. In five or six hours, if everything went well, we would reach Phnom Penh harbour.

Soon everything I had seen and that had held my attention minutes earlier disappeared. The Tonle Sap had been transformed into a sea, the horizon was a vague mush of watery grey and monsoon sky. We were now shooting out into this sea. At first stilt houses were visible near the shore and tree trunks drifted past; at some point this stopped, then there was just the maliciously glittering surface of the water and the storm-grey brooding sky, their edges melting into one another, and in the middle the *Mekong Mama* and on its roof, us. I counted, as if that were any use. There were two dozen of them with their plastic jackets snapping in the headwind; those who had enough room lay down flat so as to get some grip and not slip off if the boat were to lurch suddenly. I sat upright, bracing my heels against the miniature railing that wasn't to be trusted. He sat next to me.

The first cloudburst soon came. The sun had disappeared, sending out a garish light from its hiding-place, and we were now completely surrounded by glittering grey, from the water, from the sky; it lay on the deck, on faces. He had a tarpaulin with him, a piece of plastic sheet, black, and offered to share it with me. The storm was fierce, I didn't say no. Those who didn't have something similar were wet within seconds. First I heard him humming, the storm was tugging at the tarpaulin, he pulled it closer around us; no light came through, we sat in darkness. The rain thrashed down even harder, I felt it on my head through the plastic skin like a gentle massage. He hummed and sang, drowned out again and again by the thunderstorm, a strange song in a strange language. Then he started talking. At first I didn't understand anything. There was no beginning and no end to it. It was as if he had simply turned up the volume of the stream of speech that ran through him. At some point I realized he was talking about the taking of Phnom Penh by the Khmer Rouge. 'Après quelques jours, la ville était vide.' After a few days, the city was empty. Silent laughter followed, I could only feel his shoulders shaking quietly, we were huddled so close together. He neither smelt unpleasant nor was there anything else that was repellent about him, yet this crouching and listening was too much for me. As soon as the storm abated, I pushed the tarpaulin to one side.

～

Water still, as far as the eye could see, no shore. The sun had come back, but there was nothing sunny about it. It burnt down, and I knew that it would have burnt me by evening. Over the following days, whole strips of skin would fall off my face. The same would happen to all the whites on the roof of the boat. There weren't many of us. A businessman clinging to his attaché case. A backpacker couple, clinging to each other, realizing what they had let themselves in for, cursing themselves for not having taken the plane or some beaten-up old car along the bumpy track to Phnom Penh.

From time to time, the face of a crew member would appear over the decorative railing to check whether we were all still there. I closed my eyes against the light and when the circles of red settled, I saw the crocodiles. They hadn't stayed in their concrete pools, they were here. How could I have been so wrong, eh? I had been wrong about the passengers. For one crazy instant, I was convinced that I was sitting among crocodiles rather than in a heap of soaked, sunburnt people. I was glad when the next cloudburst came and wiped away the image. Once more my neighbour offered me his tarpaulin, again I didn't turn it down, again he hummed his song. And again he started whispering about Phnom Penh.

'The empty city, have you heard about it?'
'Yes.'

'When everyone had been driven out into the rice fields, only a small occupying force was left in Phnom Penh ...' – toneless laughter – '... and me.' His shoulders shook more violently. 'And me!'

I said nothing.

'You don't believe me? Oh, Monsieur, I saw everything. Everything, do you understand? No, you can't understand. Look, this storm right now, this crossing, this is nothing; the boat will not sink and even if it does, *tant pis*, what does it matter. A flood, a boat accident in Cambodia, a short article in the newspaper, it is nothing compared to ... that.'

'This isn't the first time you've told this story, is it?'

'What do you mean, Monsieur?' He looked taken aback for a moment, then carried on in the ironic tone of voice of someone who has seen though the person he is talking to. 'Ah! Monsieur wants an exclusive story. Nothing ready-made, eh? I'll tell you something exclusive. I will tell you about the pigs, the pigs of Phnom Penh. When they had cleared the city, they needed someone to run their errands for them. To find provisions, you see? A scavenger of the revolution. It had all happened so quickly, the bare minimum picked up, then off in columns. Lots had been left behind in the fear, in the rush, in the confusion. Furniture, supplies, all kinds of things. And not just things.' He did an imitation of pigs grunting and elbowed me in the ribs. 'They gave me a different job every day. Bring beds. Bring chickens. Bring shoes. Bring axes. Bring records. I don't know what they planned to do with the records. They hated all that stuff. Then they gave me a lorry, then people and several lorries. Bring wardrobes, bring tables, bring everything.'

The storm was now directly overhead, water washed up from under us and bounced off the roof under the tarpaulin, which was hardly any use anymore. 'Do you know what the worst thing was?' He was completely sunk in himself, in the empty city; he didn't expect an answer. 'The pigs, Monsieur, the pigs. Lots of animals had been left behind, some of them died, some of them roamed the city and gradually went wild. You seldom saw them. The domestic pigs got so wild and aggressive they attacked people.' Shaking shoulders. 'People! They attacked *me*. I was the only person wandering around the city. I often fought with pigs. I asked for a weapon. They wouldn't give me one. I said, it's dangerous, I can't go out anymore without a weapon. Then someone held a pistol to my head, and I went back out again. They were stupid. I had had a weapon for a long time already. An empty police station, not far away the empty villa of the police chief, who was out in the rice fields too. His revolver was under the floorboards in his bedroom, not a very original hiding-place for a police officer. The pigs learned incredibly quickly that their enemy was stronger than them now. I didn't kill too many, only when I needed meat, I did it like a Stone Age hunter. I had my storage places. And of course I killed them if they attacked me, but that happened less and less. We had a ceasefire, the pigs and I, I would even say a sort of peace.' We let the tarpaulin slip down; it had become pointless, we were soaked to the skin. 'Shall I tell you something, Monsieur? Those were wonderful times. I had the whole city to myself. What was Sihanouk in his palace compared to me – moi, j'étais le vrai roi de Phnom Penh!'

He didn't say another word for the rest of the crossing.

Hours and countless cloudbursts later, what looked like islands appeared, just an impression, then the outline of trees. Branches floated past, whole colonies of branches, then we saw the silhouettes of stilt houses, which soon turned into stilt houses that looked as if they were flying at half-mast in the mud-brown deluge. The boundlessness of the Tonle Sap tempered itself into a river again, still an enormously wide river but one contained by banks.

In Phnom Penh I took a room at a hotel opposite the royal palace, and when the noonday heat abated and the colours emerged, I sat by a window in the Foreign Correspondents' Club above the confluence of the Tonle Sap and the Mekong, and watched the brown water of the one merging with the green flow of the other. Someone spoke of the old days. Someone had heard about a man who had roamed the deserted streets of Phnom Penh as a sort of hunter-gatherer for the Khmer Rouge. Someone said that my hotel had been their headquarters. It seemed to me however that

– apart from the girl who organized my few things virtually invisibly – the hotel manager, a serious lady who had withdrawn to her spacious, darkened office cooled by large ventilators, and I were the hotel's only occupants, both now and since the beginning of time. I tried to imagine him receiving his orders and delivering the booty from his forays through the empty city to her there in her darkened office – sheer fantasy. When I got back, she was sitting there in the same cool twilight with the same jade-green cigarette holder in her hand, and why should it not be so and have been so forever.

Among Shamans

As I write this, rain is driving against the window; night comes early. On the table lies a necklace of hard, shrivelled-brown fruits. Once more I think: dried birds' brains. Occasionally I take them in my hand: the necklace has a certain weight and I see before me Indra, who gave it to me. His face, as it darkens with the beating of the drums, as he is carried off. It is his necklace. He wore it through those nights, wound twice around his chest; he beat the ancient leather drum, beat it faster, heading for the moment when he is seized, ridden, thrown up unbelievably high in his white shaman's robe.

When day broke, we struck our tents and climbed up and up to our midday resting place, to our overnight camp, up steep hills towards the peak, the plateau above the clouds which was said to be Shiva's home. Once a year, his disciples, the shamans, gathered there, over 4,000 metres up. Indra was a shaman. For those days and nights in the mountains close to the Tibetan border he was my friend.

⤶

The journey had begun in Copenhagen, one summer's afternoon that brought to mind happy Western images, tables under trees, voices, the sun playing on the meadow and on the skin, the opposite of the inhuman solitude of the high mountains of Central Asia. On that midsummer's day, I was pacing up and down in front of the airport counter waiting for my travelling companion, a man knowledgeable about all things shamanic and an experienced ethnologist, well-travelled and doubtless the best in this field who could have accompanied me. That is how the doctor had been recommended to me. Even if he was a little ... this is the message I got, accompanied by slightly raised eyebrows: 'A little – well, you'll see for yourself.'

Now I saw, and what I saw I would see over and over again. Wherever the doctor turned up – here in the airport terminal or later in some tiny place up in the Himalayas – people stared at him. He had not had his hair and beard cut in a long time, following the example of Shiva, the god he loved. His brown hair hung down to his shoulders, his beard to his chest. Shamans were his life's work and he didn't approach them with kid gloves. He jumped and dived right in, trying out all the things that shamans smoke, swallow, get up to, do. And his journeys for research would sometimes turn into journeys in a trance.

The two of us were supposed to fly to Nepal to find out whatever we could about shamans. The mountains there, the doctor assured me, were one of the regions of the world where this ancient practice lived on; the Amazon rainforest, which he professed to know equally well, might also be of interest. He had spent a lot of time in both. As for his homeland, he had pulled the winding key out of central European time at some stage during the seventies and happily thrown it away. He looked like a figure from the hippie years, with his silver rings and necklaces, as he strolled along the terminal corridor in the soft Danish midsummer light. By the end of this trip, he would have proved himself the most serious researcher I had ever met. Humboldt had climbed Chimborazo, Heinrich Barth penetrated into the heart of Africa. Odysseus, forefather of them all, had had himself tied to the ship's mast to listen to what no mortal might hear. He was like them. He noted, photographed, collected, picked, bought everything that came before his big, red-tinted glasses, another relic of the seventies.

Whenever he reappeared at an airport, wherever in the world it might be, he stood out due to his bulky extra luggage. He brought home important ethnological collections from his journeys, which were always journeys into the mad youth of mankind, when mortals still scrapped with gods and gods laid traps for mortal women. Between trips he wrote books. Some of these were brought out by small, esoteric publishers, others became scientific reference works. I knew none of this as I watched him approach. One thing only was immediately obvious: he was not at all your typical pale, peculiar individual coming down from his ivory tower whose hands and feet are perpetually cold. As soon as he headed towards me – athletic, suntanned, in the best of moods – and greeted me with a firm handshake, I was sure that here was my dream travelling companion. I instantly forgot everything I had heard or thought about him.

Yet there were more than enough reasons to worry about our undertaking. Much of it was hazy – everything in fact. The information about the shamans' peak: vague. The way up to it: unclear. The name of the mountain: virtually unknown, even in Kathmandu; they asked us to spell it at the office that gave out the trekking permits. And it was the same with the entire project. It had been left to us to decide whether we dared attempt the ascent to the shamans' mountain or not – it would depend on the conditions we came across. It was after all monsoon season and it would rain day and night; many paths would be impassable, we might even encounter landslides.

I had planned to decide in Kathmandu whether we would make the ascent, according to how things went with the guide that we might – maybe – meet there and with one or two shamans, who might – maybe – be prepared to talk to us. So many maybes. They all evaporated with the champagne as soon as we had reached our cruising altitude over the sea off Denmark. For the doctor had given a first demonstration of his extraordinary skills by having us both moved – our adventure would, he assured me with a grin, soon get uncomfortable enough – into Business Class, at no extra cost.

I felt cheerful, all my worries had left me, all the feverish preparations of recent weeks. I was suddenly sure that the omens were good for our trip, having seen how effortlessly the doctor had persuaded the pretty Danish ground staff to upgrade us. We were therefore in the best mood for flying, and no sooner had we raised a glass to our adventure than it was decided: to hell with monsoons, to hell with landslides and conversations in Kathmandu. Yes, we would go up the mountain and yes, after many a struggle we would stand on the summit and see it all with our own eyes.

I was amazed that I could have doubted it only half an hour earlier. I said this to him, but the doctor just said, 'Shiva Airways.' This was what it was like when you flew Shiva Airways. He himself only ever flew Shiva Airways and he could heartily recommend it. I could not have said precisely what he meant by this, but it did nothing to diminish my cheerfulness. We were as excited and silly as two boys on their first unaccompanied canoeing trip. We giggled as we asked the Danish women for more champagne, a wish they were only too glad to fulfil.

⁓

We flew into the sun and, after changing planes in Delhi in the morning, caught sight of the overcast, steaming high valley of Kathmandu in the afternoon. The hotel turned out to have been a good choice, it lay above the city. Quiet suites awaited us in the hibiscus garden. I climbed up to the roof terrace. Dusk was falling. Clouds over the city, drizzle coming down. I looked out at the jumble of houses under the monsoon sky; the damp air wafted up scents, earthy ones of mud and flowers, disturbing ones of rotting or blood. Red and yellow hibiscus grew in abundance, as did everything else here, tracks and paths were bordered by head-high hemp plants and, when I turned around, I saw Buddha's eyes above me, giant ones painted on the famous Swayambunāth stupa that towered over the Kathmandu valley. The hotel lay at their feet.

And then I heard drumming, unclear at first among the noises of the city, then more clearly. Sharp, to-tock, to-tock, not far off. Close by, someone was beating a drum with a thin, hard stick. It was the first time I had heard this monotonous, driving, riding beat. And, strangely, the hoof-beat, the image of riding came to me immediately.

As I was going down from the roof terrace, I noticed a door halfway up the stairs with a picture of a goddess on it, a cheap print. I asked a hotel employee what was behind the door.

'Lakshmi, sir.'

'The goddess of happiness lives behind that door?'

The employee shook his head in embarrassment.

'No, sir. No goddess. Lakshmi, sir.' And when I still didn't get it: 'Massage. Best massage in Kathmandu.'

I suppressed the urge to go and knock on the door immediately. I promised I would reward myself should I return from the mountain. The next morning, I visited Father McKenzie.

❧

I only had one book with me, one by the Father. Months earlier, the postman had delivered a heavy parcel of specialist literature on shamanism. But none of the authors had ever seen a shaman. They seemed not to have the slightest interest in meeting one – it might have interfered with their theories – with one exception: Father McKenzie's account. Having lived here for many years, he knew far more about these matters than any expert. I had read the body of his account of the ascent to the shamans' mountain over and over again so as not to miss the slightest detail. Yes, he had been up there, the only white man to do so; there was no other report about the mountain.

What McKenzie wrote sounded as magically

remote as a travel account from the age of the great expeditions. So it was true, the Father confirmed it: the shamans met every year on a fixed day in the lunar calendar, on a four-thousander not far from the Tibetan border, to pray for another year's Shakti, the energy that came from Shiva himself and was said to have already existed even before the younger Hindu gods entered the cosmos. Its more ancient name was Rudra, the Howler. The name is in the fruit of the rudraksha bush, which grows in the Himalayas and which is used to make the shamans' necklaces. Rudra the roamer, destroyer and creator in one, the dancer and healer and teacher of the legendary first shaman.

A gaunt man dressed in black came out to meet me in the courtyard. The hand he offered me was as cool and dry as his general appearance. Someone who had experienced many things and drawn his conclusions and made no fuss about it. His office was the same – there wasn't much to see, it was mostly silence. He had prepared some tea.

As he poured it, my gaze wandered over the bookcases that stood around us at a polite distance, like servants whose eyes nothing escapes. A light-coloured, almost primitive wooden crucifix hung on a patch of bare wall a metre or so wide, and I tried to imagine the man now asking me whether I took sugar or milk in my tea kneeling there before his lord and presenting him with the random objects he had brought back from his climbs, things from the shamans' mountains. He noticed what I was looking at, put down the sugar bowl and the milk jug and spoke as if he were simply continuing a conversation with himself that had been briefly interrupted by his guest's arrival: 'Once I gave a talk to people from back home. Protestants. They had come to evangelize India and Nepal.' He listened to this last word fade away as if it were a line from some crazy song, and a look of astonished disbelief came over his face. 'Evangelize India!' Feelings I couldn't interpret. Sympathy for the mad Protestants? Irony? Melancholia, when he thought of his own departure, of the hopes of the young priest he had once been? Evangelize India ... Maybe that was what had lured him here. 'They listened to me in silence. Then one of them stood up and said, "We are going on a spiritual war!"'

'What did you reply?'

'I hope you are well armed.'

'Father, may I ask you a question?'

'A question?'

'You never crossed the border, did you?'

He emerged from his thoughts and looked at me. 'Which border are you talking about?'

'You know more about shamans than any of the ethnologists whose books I have read. But the point is this: what happens when a shaman crosses over to beyond what we are capable of knowing and describing? You never went with them, did you? Why not?'

'No, I didn't go with them, not that far. They would have gladly taken me. They often took me to their ceremonies. Some wanted to initiate me, tell me their secrets – what they experience during their initiations and never tell a soul about. You see, I'm a scientist. I watched without commenting. When they said their mantras, I said an Our Father. That was my border, the border of my beliefs. I never crossed it.'

I thought of my Indian temple experience and said nothing. The soft tinkling of his tea-cup fetched me back. The priestly smile was there again, a little ironic, a little sad, a little lost. 'Jesus was a shaman, after a manner of speaking.' He got to his feet; this was the sign for me to leave. He accompanied me out into the hallway; we stopped to take leave of each other, but instead of saying goodbye, he picked up the train of thought I had interrupted and to which I now left him: 'Of course there is a world beyond ours. Of course there are spirits. The main question is that of evil. Evil is in the world.'

These words struck me with their biblical force. He turned away; the door into his room was ajar and a chink of light fell into the dark corridor. He pulled the door to, taking away the light with him.

⤸

The next day the doctor and I climbed the 323 steps up to Swayambunāth, to the blue eyes of the Buddha above the city, eyes of powdered lapis lazuli. Eight-year-old monks carried out their duties alongside nuns with bristly grey hair. Bells rang out, prayer wheels rattled, dogs fought over scraps, monkeys stole anything they could lay their hands on in a flash and capered away clutching their booty. The pious threw rice onto the shrines of the gods. Rich people in white shirts, with wide, red braces, arrived panting at the extremely high and extremely holy stupa.

The doctor pulled me along through the commotion and drew my attention to a stone figure the size of a child off to one side: a representation of the god Shiva, I presumed. Snakes slithered around his neck, across his chest, wound themselves around his wrists and ankles and even through the divine dancer's pierced ears. 'You're right, it's Shiva,' said the doctor, 'but of a very special kind. Shiva as a shaman. Take a good look.' A long necklace like Indra's hung around his neck, but this one was made of small human heads, not fruit; maybe it was this sight that left me with the image of birds' brains.

The doctor pointed to the instruments the god held in two of his six hands. 'This is the tantric sceptre and that is the double drum made of monkey skulls. And these here are the kapala and the kartika – the human skull bowl and the cleaver. The shamans summon the demons into this bowl, then they are smashed to bits with the cleaver, and their blood is drunk from the bowl to destroy them completely, but also so that the shamans absorb their intelligence.' The god had a demon under his dancing feet, and I thought the figure looked quite human.

Now I saw the tiny Buddha above Shiva's head. An idea suddenly occurred to me, a nice little theory I hoped would impress the doctor. 'The path of mankind represented by a statue, from the beginning of all religion, the magical antidote to demons and disaster, to the highest degree of spirituality – 10,000 years from the pounding feet of the old shepherd god to the motionless spirit meditating above his brow.'

The doctor smiled. 'Nice idea. From the stupid, superstitious shamans of mankind's infancy up to the wise Buddha-Jesus. Let's make a deal: no more theories until we're up on the mountain.'

'I'll try my best. Theories won't get us to the top.'

On our seventh morning in Kathmandu, a brightly coloured, dented bus pulled up and, once their luggage had been loaded and lashed to the roof, about two dozen men climbed in and spread themselves out over the seats. This was the bus that would take us to just this side of the border. Our rash plan in Business Class had grown into a 23-strong expedition. Most of these were porters. They would carry everything that needed to be hauled up the mountain on their backs. Tents against the rain along with poles and other equipment, blankets against the cold, torches against the dark, the cooking tent, sacks of rice, potatoes, vegetables and whatever else we needed.

The porters were wiry men from the Sherpa tribe, plainly and sometimes poorly clothed, almost all of them barefoot. They were in a good mood and were looking forward to this trip, which seemed quite easy to them; they were used to very different altitudes and privations up there in the ice. Mohan, the guide, had hired 17 men, as well as a cook and the kitchen boy. Mohan himself was a nimble little man who didn't look his 60 years. While we had been on daytime outings and kept Indra company at night during his rituals, he was the one who had put the expedition together – done the shopping, chosen the people, planned and calculated. Mohan was the brains of the party, everywhere at once like a sheepdog and always ready with a ribald joke. In short, he was a man I could trust. And Indra was with us. Anyone who didn't know him would have taken him for a normal city-dweller with his ironed trousers, his glasses, wedding ring and his smooth face. A bank employee in Kathmandu perhaps, on the way to see relatives in the mountain village he called home.

One person wasn't in the bus – Mai. Her life bore some similarities to Indra's. Like him she came from a remote village, like him she had become a shaman when she was young, like him she had tried in vain to escape her fate. Over the previous nights they had both drummed themselves into that other world that was merely a fascinating assertion to me, but to Mai and Indra was as real as Kathmandu with its temples and its hippie quarter Thamel, the swarms of flies over freshly butchered meat and Buddha's blue eyes watching over everything.

They had taken the utmost care only to reach for their drums for a good reason – if a person who was sick or struck by some other affliction requested their help. Yet they had really been doing it for us. They travelled by night so that they could report back to us day after day on what they had seen. Was Mai a beautiful woman? Not one who turned heads. But when she went into a trance, yes, then she was beautiful. She was a shaman of rare powers, I had heard people say of her, and this was attributed to the unusual initiation she had received – her knowledge had not, as was generally the case, been passed on by her father but by a being from that other world. Europeans would have called this a fairytale, a childish delirium. Mai laughed when I told her this. For her, everything was as real as could be – her awakening, her life. I could see she was special. Others went into a trance; she ran into it like a child running to its father. I told her that too. She answered no, not to her father, she was running to that being, 'to my guru'. It was her element, it transformed her into a Mai I couldn't take my eyes off. She didn't want to make the long climb with us, but she had promised to be at the sacrificial feast on the mountain, taking a shorter route.

~

The bus crossed umpteen passes. Again and again it went up and down through hairpin bends, and I was overcome by a strange satisfaction every time we scaled a pass and hung for a moment at the highest point between ascent and descent. Sometimes, when a landslide had buried the road, and both man and bus had to work their way across the scree, the driver was forced to perform much-applauded tricks.

The afternoon light was already fading as we reached our destination, the last marketplace before Tibet, a row of garage-like shops to the left and right of the road, nothing else. The drizzle that had been with us all journey increased to a downpour as soon as we got out. While the sherpas unloaded our luggage and divided it up between them, Mohan ran off to buy umbrellas and came back with both arms full of them, cheap Chinese goods like most things on this market at the end of the world. I looked around. Everyone had disappeared into the shop caves; everybody holed up out of the rain for as long as possible. It looked as if our enterprise was unravelling before it had even begun. Suddenly, however, at a sign from Mohan, the column assembled as if out of nothing and, seconds later, he disappeared sideways between two shops against the slope. We leapt after him, one after the other, our umbrellas held low over our heads. The path immediately climbed steeply uphill.

We walked until it got dark and, still fresh, maintained our original skipping rather than striding tempo. The porters laughed and chatted, as if they had finally been let off the leash. We occasionally met mountain people. An old man on thin, brown legs; a clucking noise came from the bag he carried. A girl, barefoot, her back-basket full of maize. Families were carrying their crops down into the valley, their heads bent forwards, a back-basket hanging from every headband. Giant bales of maize straw on two legs came towards us. There were still some stone benches to rest on here, long ones built across the slope. If Mohan allowed them to rest, the sherpas leaned back against these benches and rested their load on them for a few minutes. Hordes of cicadas made their noise, and against this background, more and more clearly as we went on, there was a stamping sound that seemed to come from the bowels of the earth. When we rested, it drowned out and took on our pulse; when we set off, it urged us on. Sweat ran down my face, down my neck, down my chest and mixed in with the rain.

For a while we followed the gold river, which owed its name to the stones that once shone in it. After an earthquake, said Mohan, the shining in the river had disappeared.

'When was that?'

'Only recently, about a hundred years ago.'

At dusk we reached a small Shiva temple, which Mohan had intended as our resting place for the first night. The god's symbol, the trident, stood out black against the grey sky. The tents were quickly pitched, and straw beds were prepared for the doctor and myself in a barn. The rain stayed.

We continued steeply uphill on the second day as well. The water now came from above us and below us as the path we had followed up to this point left us; again and again we headed straight up the mountain, and we climbed up roaring mountain streams more often than paths, jumping from stone to stone without so much as a glance at the woods and mountains, for we had to take care over every step and the stones and rocks in the stream were extremely slippery. I was glad that I had followed a whim and put on deck shoes; I had no others with me. They were perfect for a climb that was as slippery as a ship's deck.

The rain didn't stop falling. It was the last thing I heard before I fell asleep dog-tired, it was the first noise when I woke up in my one-man tent and looked forward to the soon-familiar second morning sound. The kitchen boy scratched at my tent and, as softly as possible and as loudly as necessary, forcefully whispered his wake-up call: 'Morning, sir! Morning tea!'

Another ritual rounded off each day: in the twilight, after we had put up our tents in the pouring rain a few hundred metres higher up, I removed my deck shoes and checked how many leeches had bored holes into my feet that day, and how many holes blood was seeping out of. Was it three or four or ten?

The sherpas had made a poison against leeches

from wild tobacco mixed with something else they wouldn't divulge, torn up a piece of cloth into equal-sized strips, filled them with the poultice, tied them up into little bags and handed them out to everyone. I couldn't imagine when they had done this, for they carried our load all day, then when darkness fell they ate and settled down to sleep, if they weren't spending the whole night with Indra. But suddenly there were 23 bags of fresh leech poison, each of them hanging from a little stick so that they looked from afar like the bundles gnomes carry in children's stories, but from close up like the blackish-brown, cotton tea bags you find in student kitchens. The poison had a guaranteed and fatal effect, the sherpas said. If we found a leech, we only had to touch it with the bag and it would drop off us, dead. And it was true. We tried it over and over again, and it worked every time.

To anyone who saw us or could have seen us from a distance, we must have made for an odd sight. A straggling procession in the rain, each of us plodding along on his own holding the stick with the poison sachet in one hand and an open umbrella – already quite battered after a couple of days – in the other. From time to time, someone would slap his poison bag against his leg, the sherpas nonchalantly and routinely, myself deliberately, astonished every time that it really did work. Leech after leech dropped off me, as if touched by magic. There was still the darkness of my deck shoes; they crept inside and had the whole day to tap into a nice, fat vein and drink their fill because you felt nothing. It was only when I took off my shoes in the evening that I would notice the penny-sized boreholes in my feet and extract the sated leeches.

Every evening some of the sherpas' poison was spread in a magic circle around each tent. However the circle must have been sprinkled a little carelessly once; I turned over to switch off the torch and go to sleep and found a leech right in front of me, stretching out hungrily towards me, feeling around for me, for a good place, swollen with excitement, as thick as my finger.

On the third day, we had an encounter that was to have far-reaching consequences. We were taking our lunch break at a drinks stall when a couple appeared from the direction in which we would continue and drew all eyes to them – and this wasn't only because we seldom met anyone up here now and we were the only guests at the stall. The two of them were of slender, even delicate build, and of their age I can only say that they were getting on, no longer young. Both of them had handsomely furrowed faces, both of them were wearing close-fitting, ankle-length red robes. Our people knew them. They bowed to them. The two of them received these demonstrations of respect reluctantly and dispassionately, proof that these were nobles. A couple of barefooted wanderers, unconcerned by appearances such as their clothes having holes in them here and there as well as other marks of their travels. No question about it: to judge by his clothing, he was a shaman, and no minor one. Indra seemed to know him too; he treated him in a manner that indicated the greatest respect. As soon as I got a chance, I asked Indra about him. 'He is the most powerful,' he said. 'Incidentally, do you know what these mountains are called?'

I said the name I'd seen on the map.

'Yes, that's what's written on your trekking permit. I mean its real name: Jhankriland. Jhankri means shaman in the Sherpa language, and this man is their most respected Jhankri.'

We invited both of them to eat and drink with us. He accepted with the polite condescension of someone who expects nothing less. The conversation was held in his language; I sat to one side and observed him. He had let a single lock of hair grow long; it hung from the back of his head right down to the bottom of his back, a sign of his love for Shiva, the doctor explained to me in a whisper, 'the god who wears his hair long and wild'.

His wife sat close beside him. The two of them looked like a pair of young lovers on their travels. She looked at him often and smiled when he spoke. He spoke in more modulated tones than simple hill farmers, although he was undoubtedly one himself; he generally spoke quietly so that everyone had to lean towards him, then suddenly passionately and firmly like someone who is used to people listening to what he says. Mohan and Indra offered him *bidis* to smoke and chang to drink, a brownish, frothy beer-like brew that was passed around in bowls. They advised me not to try the Tibetan beer. 'It'd make you ill,' said Mohan, raised the bowl to his lips and took a swig.

Once we had exchanged these courtesies, our guest told us what he had experienced ten minutes before. All of a sudden, a large snake had lain across the path. 'We were on our way to Dudh Kunda.' A holy lake the colour of milk, explained Mohan, who was translating for me. 'All these years, I have gone up to the top of Shiva's mountain; this year I wanted to go to Dudh Kunda. I asked the snake to let me pass. It did not move. I grew angry, pulled out my knife and wanted to kill it. Then I thought to myself, stop, no, this means something. I walked around the snake and ten minutes later I meet you!' Now he could see what the snake had wanted of him. 'I will go up the mountain with you, if you don't mind.'

I meant to ask him some questions. I had read in Father McKenzie's account that fights occasionally broke out on the mountain between enemy shamans and their followers. He waved this aside. 'Don't worry, leave that to me. All the shamans up there are my pupils.' He sat there, upright and ready to go, and gave instructions about the sacrificial animals that would need to be bought along the way and taken up to the mountain. 'They have to be female goats; the mountain is a female deity.'

'Ask him,' I said turning to Mohan, 'to tell us about what he does as a Jhankri.' The doctor advised against it. 'He'll avoid the question. He doesn't like talking about it. They are initiated healers; that's why they guard their secrets, that's why they are so shy. If you ask a real shaman whether he is one, he'll always say, oh no, I don't know much about that. If someone boasts of all the things he can do, then he can't do anything, then he's a *chicken shaman*. Someone who tries to con tourists with a few cheap tricks.' I urged Mohan to translate my question and it turned out exactly as the doctor had said it would. The little anxious shaman prince reacted defensively. 'He doesn't want to talk about himself,' said Mohan. 'He says to come and see.'

Come and see. He'd been with us only an hour and he was already doing the inviting. Our expedition ended here – or at least the part we had been leading, Mohan, the doctor and myself. Now the shaman was leading us. We were passing through Jhankri country – his country. He was king here. Soon there would be ten or twelve men in red and white clothing at the front of the column, with crowns of feathers on their heads, necklaces and bells around their chests, beating the shaman's drum. More and more of them joined us the higher we climbed – or joined him, rather. It was as if a magnet had been placed in our group – him. The news that the old man was going up the mountain preceded us; in every hamlet and on every mountain pasture, they were expecting us. I checked my map and reckoned that by now we had reached an altitude of 3,500 metres. There was still enough vegetation around to feed the scattered settlements of hill farmers and their livestock – cattle, goats and, increasingly, yaks.

～

Mohan had announced that the next morning's climb would be particularly steep. And so it turned out. As if we had sworn some oath to avoid complicated hairpins from now on, we climbed straight uphill, sometimes through torrents, sometimes over moss-covered steps, always through the mountain forests. I first gave up paying any heed to our surroundings, then to the path. I shrank into my breath, which had dwindled to an intermittent panting; I staggered upwards, further, further, another step, I pushed myself higher and higher, and clung onto my panting like a rope. One of the sherpas, a strongly built, young man, gestured that he would take my rucksack. He stood out. He never looked tired, nothing was too heavy for him, he would willingly shoulder one and a half times his load. He would set off with a smile when the others were savouring every last minute of the rest they were allowed; now he saw how I was panting, looked back at me, stopped more regularly to give me encouragement, and finally offered to carry my rucksack in addition to his far heavier load. I thanked him and refused; I still had my pride.

A little later, I realized that I wouldn't be able to carry on for much longer. It must have been about noon we reached a meadow and Mohan let us rest; it was the first level spot since early light. A Buddhist temple stood there, the door lintel bearing a Tibetan inscription. The higher we climbed, the more Tibetan it became. The chortens along the path, the faces, the names. The people we met were called Sherpa, Tamang, Gurung. Tribes of Tibetan origin. Chortens, inscriptions, people; everything was swirling around in my head. The world had gone black and red before my eyes. I remember seeing the sherpas getting down to work without the slightest sign of fatigue, setting up the field kitchen, gathering firewood, peeling potatoes. I had stretched out on the stone step of the little temple and fell into a deep and leaden sleep.

I had no idea how long I had been lying there when I very slowly came to, through layers of blackness. I did not come empty-handed. There was an image before my eyes, a figure, somewhat larger than a man, some-what blurred, sitting by me as if at someone's sickbed or even deathbed, but not threatening, just there, half turned away so that, to my regret, I could not make out his face – for he was male. And yet at the same time I was afraid to look into this face.

I sensed, even now as I awoke, that someone was

there. Could it be that the figure was still with me, that it had come with me out of the blackness? I opened my eyes and looked at the concerned, furrowed face that I had observed so often since that first meeting at the drinks stall. It was he who sat by my side, the little red barefoot king.

I raised my head and saw that the midday meal had long been eaten and everything packed away again; the porters sat or stood around the meadow, looking over at us, and I realized that they were waiting for me. I sat up. The old man nodded with satisfaction and said something to Mohan, who was standing next to him. 'He says, you're fine, you will soon regain your strength; we can carry on.' Everyone seemed relieved at the shaman's words, and the sherpas pulled on the loads lying ready for our onward march. Less than five minutes later and the column began to move. I asked Mohan how long I had been lying there.

'A good two hours. We were worried; you couldn't hear us, you were totally gone. He was with you.' He pointed to the shaman. 'He spoke mantras and never once left your side.' Now I remembered the last thing that had happened before I fell asleep. He had come over to me and whispered things I didn't understand, accompanied by sweeping, circular movements and smoke.

I stood up and it was just as he had said. My first few steps were unsteady, but a few minutes later I could keep up with the set pace, even though the climb was as steep as before. We had made good progress that morning, said Mohan, and he didn't insist on resuming our forced march. After half an hour, I was striding out as if nothing had happened. I no longer thought about my exhaustion, only about the image with which I had emerged from the blackness.

As we sat eating roast potatoes and chicken that evening, I went over to the shaman and told him, with Mohan's help, about the figure I had seen. He listened without taking his eyes off me. Several times he asked a question. Mohan had to translate word for word. He said something.

'What was that, Mohan? What did he say?'

'You saw Shiva – he was the black figure. You were afraid to see him uncovered and at the same time you wanted to. That is how it is with men and gods. We want to be close to them and yet we are afraid of them, and rightly so. Seeing him would have killed you. He came very close to you and yet he protected you from being burnt by him. That is why he covered himself. Shiva likes you.'

The old man in his red robe was glowing with joy. So close! His god had been so close. The doctor, who had listened in on everything, took it upon himself to share the shaman's joy. I was grateful to him for that. I stepped to one side and made it look as if I were deeply moved, and I was moved in a way, only by whom or by what I didn't know. I had won the heart of the old man of the mountains; his god had judged me worthy of his help, the old howler and healer; with his blessing, he had healed a stranger on the meadow that noon. He had almost revealed himself. This complete stranger had almost seen what he, the powerful shaman, saw on his night-time journeys. Everything about this confused me. He wasn't my god. It was his god, his country. Could you visit a god like you could visit a country?

The doctor and I had spoken little recently. He kept to the shamans; by day he climbed with them, at night he was with them when they went into a trance. I didn't hold it against him if he preferred their company; he was a researcher and these days and nights were a rare opportunity for him to delve further into a subject that fascinated him. Yet I never lost sight of him. Even in the fog and the clouds, he was always visible in his bright-red, tight-fitting, knee-length cycling shorts and his colourful T-shirts with psychedelic record sleeve designs from the seventies or six-armed Shiva-Rudra printed on them. We must have looked a strange couple to the sherpas and hill farmers, all of whom were too polite to be caught whispering about or glancing sideways at these two, the tall long-haired one in his red shorts and his shaven-headed companion in the ungainly deck shoes.

Then I suddenly saw the doctor throw up his arms. The sherpas stood still too, pointed ahead, called out to one another. The peak had levelled out into a plateau, a wide mountain meadow; but because we were all walking in loose formation, it was some time before I reached the spot and realized what had brought the column to a halt. The plateau was a royal box; the view it offered was captivating. The gigantic mountains in the sunlight. Everything was brightly lit, the valleys were steaming. At last we saw where we were; at last, after days in the rain, the fog, the clouds, I saw the Himalayas. The veils we had just been walking through had been torn aside, and the highest peaks in the world showed themselves in a light that had us shouting with delight – for the people from the mountains, here were the gods showing themselves.

'Look, that's Manaslu!'

'And Annapurna over there!'

An overwhelming but fleeting sight. They covered themselves over again as quickly as they had appeared, and we walked through clouds and water. It came from all sides.

Less and less frequently, we would pass a house in which men and animals lived under the same roof, but the residents had unfailingly erected their pious barricades: a small altar by the path, a sacrifice in a woven basket – rice, maize, mint, flowers and, in the centre, a clay cone with a wick in it. It represented the world mountain Meru, including the axis of the world and four red flowers showing the points of the compass. I thought the wicks and sticks jutting out of the cones looked like antennae, primitive but robust antennae. Strange devices for mysterious purposes. This is how, I thought to myself, the first conquistadors must have passed through Mexico and Venezuela and Peru, through a continent of alien objects and signs. This was what it must be like walking through Tokyo all on your own. When we neared a house, a welcoming table awaited us outside. Frothy Tibetan beer and a request to the shamans to stay the night; someone was in urgent need of their help. Often it was a fever that refused to go away, inexplicable, mysterious paralysis or pains. Mohan grinned. 'Or women who've gone mad. You know, typical shaman illnesses.'

As night billowed up out of the valleys like smoke – valleys that lay 1,000 or 2,000 metres below us, we had now been walking above the clouds for a long time – we came to three houses and accepted their occupants' invitations. Exhausted from the climb, I fell asleep immediately after I'd been shown to a narrow wooden bed in one of the houses. At some point I was woken by a shrill, piercing sound.

It was the depths of night. There must have been animals in here: a pungent smell of wet wool and urine. The same deathly sound again, made from blowing through something I imagined to be terrifying – the sound bored its way into my brain. I jumped up, grabbed hold of the woollen blanket I'd been lying under, wrapped myself in it and groped my way to the door. The night was pitch-black outside as well. Not a star in the sky, no sky at all. There was something going on in the next house, light was shining through a chink; I walked towards it, found the rough wooden door, slowly pulled it open. A low room. Walls made of stones all around, soot-stained beams supporting the shingle roof with tools and back-baskets hanging from them; the floor was of tamped earth, blotchy and greasy with trampled and spilt matter. In the middle of the room a fire was burning.

No one noticed me, everyone was enthralled by what was taking place. I recognized a few of our sherpas as well as Indra, Mohan and the doctor; the others must have been people from the hamlet. In the middle of the circle they formed, next to the fire, the mask was dancing. Its dark-red eyes were bulging, black and red-brown yak hair hung down from it, its bared teeth were a rotten yellow as if they had been buried for a long time – a face come back from the grave. It was larger than life, but was worn by a man. His head and chest were completely hidden by the mask, by the ancient, terrifying face. There was no doubt that it was the old shaman king who was bearing it and this word was exactly right; he bore it like a burden. It bent him double. He served the mask, and his service made it seem strangely alive. Whenever it came dancing closer, the circle shrank back. Was I oversensitive to the horror of this because I'd woken up so suddenly? Perhaps. Yet what I saw was not a man who this once put on a mask like a hat that he would then take off again. A creature was giving birth to itself before my eyes, and this birth was voracious. I was watching the masked demon devour the old shaman. It had already gobbled up the upper body; it still needed the scampering lower body for as long as the dance lasted, before finally swallowing up the old man entirely. I glanced at the doctor; he was as spellbound by the dance as I was. What was he thinking? Now he looked round as if searching for something; our eyes met, there was a hint of a grin and a shake of the head, then he was once more in thrall to the scene by the fire.

I turned to watch it too, the slightly built man under the mask. Under the yoke. For that's what it was: a yoke, a holy yoke I grant you. Someone from the village, selected to give up his normal life, to serve the village as a living membrane stretched between this world and the other. Now I saw what a shaman was, I saw it in front of me. It was a burden, a duty, a human sacrifice. The aim of this night-time dance was to give birth, over and over again, to a messenger, half man, half non-man, who served the village on the one hand and the demons on the other when they met to negotiate. The village fed off its shaman, just as the mask fed off the person wearing it. With him, it came alive. Set aside, it was just a piece of wood. They had been woken in the night by the man into whose old, loving eyes into which I had already looked once today when he brought me back from the blackness during the stop at the mountain meadow. It was he who had blown the shrill death trumpet that had woken me just before – who else.

Someone handed it to him now. He took it in both hands, spoke to it, blew on it, came towards me. I moved out of his way, pushed open the door I was leaning on, and realized as I stumbled out that this was nothing to do with me. He didn't even see me. The ritual dance was over. Now for the main event. Everyone followed the shaman outside. He walked past me and disappeared out of the light from the open door, and I heard that sound again. He held up the flute, it gleamed white in the night; he held it up to the mouth of the mask, and blew.

'The thigh-bone trumpet.' It was the doctor speaking; he stood beside me now. 'Consider yourself lucky. There are very few people in the world who are not from these mountains who have heard a shaman blow the bone flute.'

'A human bone?'

'Of course.'

'What's he going to do?'

'There's a burial place here, where the dead are buried in the traditional Tibetan way. They are hacked to pieces. That's where he's going now. Demons love those places. There, he'll take off his clothes and summon the demons with the thigh-bone trumpet, naked, wearing only the mask and holding the phurba, Shiva's weapon, the thunderbolt, and fight them.'

'Why, in heaven's name. Just for the sake of fighting?'

'The people here have asked him to. Disease, madness, their livestock are dying. He asks: Has anyone died recently? They answer: Yes, so-and-so. He says: It is the ghost of the dead person that is tormenting you. The ghost will not go where it belongs. He will say to him: Go, you no longer belong here. The ghost will refuse. They will fight. That is how it always is. A great deal of misfortune hangs over this house. Now do you understand how lucky we are?'

'Who says he'll win the fight?'

'No pain, no gain!' The doctor gave a hearty surfer's laugh.

'You see this as a kind of sport, do you?'

'A little bit, yes. But don't worry – this isn't the first time he's done this. And he's got the mask. Even I have never seen such a powerful mask before. It can kill demons. There aren't many who can wear it; out of maybe 100 shamans hereabouts, he's the only one who owns a mask like this. No, he won't be defeated tonight.'

The mask walked away, the people followed it as far as they dared, then they turned back, awe and fear written on their faces. He was their last hope, the man who now went towards the dead to wrestle with god knows what. Nobody went home, nobody slept. We sat in the sooty cave house, and the conversation with the doctor got underway again, whispers in the silence of this house so far away from the houses we knew.

He had experienced all this early on, he said, when he was still an ethnology student. 'Experienced, you understand, not heard or read about it.' He talked of an initiatory experience under the influence of a substance

133

whose name I have forgotten. 'I was looking down at myself and watched my body being cut up, completely cut up. My flesh peeled off, my skeleton shattered, my ego scattered to the four winds. And then, when there was nothing left of me, I was put back together again. That is what they go through when they become shamans, sometimes when they are kids of only nine or ten. Everyone here has gone through it. Indra over there. And the tall one next to him.'

'The dancer?'

'Yes, the dancer. Crazy guy.'

A remarkably lanky shaman was leaning against the wall beside Indra. The two had become friends; they were inseparable in their red-and-white shaman's robes, with their necklaces, drums, feather crowns. We called him the dancer because he had greeted us in his village with quick, daring leaps. This was his way; he didn't walk, he danced in a trance, a wiry man with lively eyes; in the West he would have become an actor. His impulsiveness, his bony face that was always on the point of breaking into a whinny of laughter reminded me of the Don Camillo films of my childhood, of the war between the crafty Catholic priest Camillo and the Communist mayor Peppone in an Italian village. There was no war like that here. There was no need for actors here. Here, both characters merged into one and the same person: the dancer was mayor of his mountain village and village shaman at once, Don-Camillo-and-Peppone in the Himalayas. And the best thing of all was that he had joined us immediately and with great enthusiasm.

'Crazy guy,' the doctor repeated. 'You should have seen him last night. He took burning wicks and swallowed them as if they were cough sweets. You shouldn't sleep at night; you can catch up in Kathmandu.' He looked at me. 'You're brooding again.'

'Yes, about you. If you've experienced that type of initiation, then you must be a shaman yourself.'

He shook his head, a little regretfully I thought. 'No, I don't know. I've been there, often in fact, I can easily go into a trance – like this.' He clicked his fingers and nodded at Indra and the others. 'You don't even have to be a shaman, by the way. Did you know that you can take someone with you?'

'Like riding pillion on a motorbike?'

'Something like that, yes. I often travel with someone.'

'I can already see the advert. Trance trips in Nepal! Get on! And we're off! You know, I've considered it.'

'Really? Brooding as ever, were you? You've already got a few bumps at the thought of it – there.' He touched my forehead. It did actually feel quite bumpy.

'McKenzie's right,' I continued, 'it's always the same struggle – between a man and his demons.'

'Ah, so this is where the Church comes into it.'

'If all that exists – another world, ghosts, demons – maybe we've simply lost our ear for it.'

'You're making progress.'

'Slowly. Why then are these ghosts, well ... so local? It's puma ghosts in Peru. Tiger ghosts here. It might be squirrel ghosts in Germany. One kind of shepherd cult here, another shepherd cult there. It's very site-specific, isn't it? Not universal.'

'Go on.'

'Perhaps McKenzie never went with the shamans on their trance journeys because he felt it would have been like a relapse. I think he likes them, I even think he buys their stories of what they see on the other side. Of course there are spirits. Monotheists like him don't dispute that. They understand the demon-killers with a thunderbolt, crown of feathers and drum as some kind of older and at the same time younger cousins, who fight evil with magical, Bronze Age weapons.'

'You can't help yourself, can you? Fitting everything you see into the familiar system. Now you're starting with that religious evolution stuff again. From primitive shamanism upwards to the spirituality of the high religions. The Father seems to have made quite an impression on you. I want to tell you something …'

We talked and talked. The children had long fallen asleep on their mother's laps or in a corner which the firelight did not reach, and many a man dozed as he crouched or leaned against a wooden pillar until, at some point, there was movement. Someone leapt to the door, pushed it open, and outside stood the small, old king carrying the red mask in both hands in front of him. He entered, paid no heed to anyone, put the mask down carefully, knelt down and prayed. After perhaps half an hour, he got up, covered the mask and gave some brief instructions. A chicken was caught – the chickens were crouching among the people, asleep like us – an altar was erected and the ritual began; a knife flashed, blood flowed, the chicken twitched and took its final steps, and when it lay still, the shamans bent over it to draw their conclusions from its position and other signs.

When this was over and the diagnosis had been announced to the anxious, hopeful hill farmers, exhaustion overtook the old man. He slumped, his face ashen. His wife had been by his side since he had entered the hut. She took him by the hand, led him to the back of the room and made a bed for his head on her lap. He hardly noticed, lay in her arms like a dead man. I thought of the doctor's initiation, of his tale of his physical dismembering. This was how the old man looked now, as if a ghost or god would have to put him back together again. This is when my thoughts frayed – all of us must have felt the same. As if a power source had suddenly been turned off, we fell asleep where we were.

Mohan woke us up, it was already light. He called us a bunch of old wives who couldn't cope with a big night anymore, and made lots of noise. I went across to the house in which I should actually have slept; there the woman first gave the calf that I had smelt in the darkness some food, then she gave me a plate of lentils. The calf lived under the same roof as the people, and I soon realized that I had sat down within its spraying radius. It was well-fed and sprightly and dragged its tail brush through its own damp excrement, waved it around, flicked and hit the edge of my plate. I wiped the spattered excrement away like raindrops, carried on eating, and was surprised at my indifference.

Mohan drove us up the path. He said that today was the last day, we would reach the peak and we would have to, because at sunrise tomorrow the sacrificial feast would begin. Tomorrow – that was how close we were to the day for which we had toiled so hard. Yesterday the path had run almost level along the edge of woods, a stroll. Today we had to cover the last few hundred metres of altitude, another tough climb. Mohan and I had been walking together for a while when he pointed discreetly to the sherpa I had also noticed.

'You see him? Always out in front, always in a good mood, always an extra ten kilos. So what do you think of him?'

'Out with it. You know, I can tell from your face.'

'Of course I know. I watched him, then I asked him to explain himself. I say, what's wrong with you, you can't fool me! He admitted it straight away. A hidden shaman. Yes, that's right, he says, but don't give me away or else they'll put pressure on me and it'll start all over again. He just wants some peace and to earn some money for his family.'

Then Mohan gave me a lecture about how poor the shamans were. His father had been one too. He could be called to a distant mountain farm at any moment, then all-night rituals. 'And a bag of rice by way of thanks. I know many people who run away from their vocation and go underground in Kathmandu.' He smiled. 'You know one too.'

'Yes, him over there.'

'I don't mean him. I'm talking about Indra. Ask him yourself.'

I caught up with Indra, and he confirmed it all. Yes, he had run away from his mountain village to Kathmandu and become a policeman.

'You're a policeman?'

'I was. Good job. It worked until someone from my village turned up in our unit and went around telling everyone who I was. No sooner did my company officer hear about it than he summoned me and sent me to see his wife to heal her melancholia. I healed her, and it started all over again.'

'And?'

'You can see what happened. I've accepted my fate, what else was I supposed to do? I obviously can't escape it. I quit the police service.'

The dancer caught up with us, he was looking for Indra's company. It was fine by me. I dropped back; the path was getting narrow as it was. Let the column move on. Watch as it loosened, half-dissolved, strung out. The path led along an incredibly steep escarpment. How quiet everything had gone here. No noisy mountain torrent, no sherpa calls and their echoes, not even the screech of a bird. Thirty men in loose formation, brightly dressed, chalk-coloured, a pretty line of moving white dots against a soaring stone-grey slope that dropped steeply.

The front of the line had been held up. The pretty line bunched together into a knot; something had happened or was threatening to happen. 'A landslide!' The word flew from man to man, and the one who caught it and shouted it on lent it a seriousness that I not seen before in the sherpas. I reached the knot and saw what had caused it. The landslide was a scree slope, as wide as a football pitch but much longer. We couldn't tell how far down it reached, how far down the slope went, only how mountain and landslide disappeared into the fog below us. The escarpment towered several hundred metres above us. The drop might have been 2,000 metres or more. Over on the other side of the landslide, I saw Mohan giving his orders and waving energetically between two boulders. Come on! Next one! No dawdling, come on, come on!

Each of us paused for a moment by the edge of

the river of scree, gathered himself and ran or hopped across as nimbly and as fast as possible, intent only on getting over. On the other side, outstretched hands awaited him and pulled him in behind the cliff from where those of us who still had to face the danger were keenly watched, and guided and encouraged with stifled shouts. There would be no stopping, no salvation for anyone who took one false step and set the scree rolling. And should anyone attempt to jump to the aid of a flailing man as he plunged into the valley below, they would be lost as surely as he.

Now it was my turn. I faced it and saw how unsafe the scree really was, as loose as the freshly excavated earth of a molehill. The river of soil and stones looked as if it had been halted in its fall, as if this unnatural frozen state might end at any moment and the scree slope start moving again, clattering at first, then rattling, rolling, roaring. It would take very little human weight to set it off. A foot on the wrong stone, and the mountain would sweep everything away with it.

Suddenly the doctor was standing next to me. I had thought I was last in line and hadn't noticed that he was walking quite some way behind me. Not a word was spoken. He was looking at the field of scree. He saw what I saw – the way the scree was now meant it could be a matter of life and death which one of us ventured across first and which second. Mohan was waving almost angrily from behind his cliff: Go! Go! It was an order; we followed it like synchronized swimmers. One hand outstretched, we caught hold of the other's hand, walked out into the river of earth and stone, hopped across on tiptoe. Mohan stretched as far as he could towards us, his face twisted. He caught hold of us, pulled us in behind the cliff, hugged us. I didn't look back. For the rest of the day, the doctor and I walked next to each other. There was no need for words.

⌐

We reached the summit at dusk. No tree nor bush grew there, only hard grass in the wind. The summit was shaped like two humps of unequal size; the real shrine was the plateau at the top of the higher one. We would only set foot on it tomorrow morning. Mohan instructed the sherpas to set up camp on the slopes of one of the slightly lower secondary summits like the other groups of pilgrims that had arrived before us. And new groups appeared as our people pitched the tents and prepared everything for the night. It was strange, after so many days spent marching through uninhabited wilderness, to come across such a large and busy camp. People were cooking, eating and drinking all around. There was little indication of what awaited us. Had it not been for the shamans with their drums and bells and feather crowns, one might have thought there was a midsummer night's picnic going on at the top of this four-thousander.

My tent was quickly pitched, and I didn't want to wait for food, I wasn't hungry. I wanted to go to Shiva's site for as long as the approaching night allowed. A path led through the dip between the two peaks; it soon reached some steps. Now I could see above me the iron footbridge Mohan had talked about. It spanned a small gorge. The footbridge was in filigree against the darkening sky, an unexpected image up here as we had hardly seen a single man-made object for days. I climbed up the steps, reached the iron footbridge, which turned out to be wobbly, and picked my way across.

Shiva's place of worship was a flat plateau about 30 metres long and about half as wide. There were several shrines. The largest was a hill of rust and spikes, a thicket of iron – lots of tridents. Shiva's symbol, dragged up to 4,000 metres, thrown onto this pious pile over centuries, if not far longer.

There was nothing to suggest that I would get to see the gigantic mountains all around the next day. The ice-grey gods veiled themselves. Standing facing them on this peak, not their equal but nevertheless granted an audience, they did not reveal themselves. Thick clouds screened the wonders of Tibet. Night fell, I clambered back across the footbridge and down the steps. Halfway to the camp stood the pilgrim hostel; before I had walked past it, this time I went in. It was a plain two-storey building, a shell in fact; anything more would have been a waste. Like everything else up here – bridge, steps, shrines – the pilgrim hostel was used only once a year. For this one night, however, it was overcrowded. Hill folk were camped here, clustered around their shamans and waiting for sunrise and the sacrificial feast.

Inside the house, I saw Indra. I knew what was coming, it was just starting; Indra was drumming the *Calling Mantra*, to-tock, to-tock, he was calling his guru, and this guru was not of this world. He would soon start beating it faster, more impellingly; this is what happened now – the *Travelling Mantra* for the journey to the other side. He was sitting on the concrete floor, his legs folded under him, and he was now thrown into the air, as I had often seen happen, a few centimetres, without doing anything other than drum. It looked hydraulic. I couldn't explain this phenomenon, which seemed to make a mockery of gravity. Indra would have had to have huge leg muscles to propel himself into the air from a sitting position. He wasn't frail, but he wasn't a trained sportsman either. And I had seen old shamans, nothing but skin and bones, jump in the same way.

Indra's eyes were shut. His light, smooth face grew stern, a mask, as if life were draining out of him. The bells were jingling, he was being shaken, his legs began to tremble, the tremors spread to his whole body. And then, amid hissed and spat exclamations of 'Hosh! Hosh!', he shot across. Indra was here. Indra was gone. No one took their eyes off him, off what remained of him here. Thoughts rushed through my mind. Yes, I liked him and wanted to believe him. No, he wasn't fooling me. Yes, I could see it. No, I couldn't see anything at all. I didn't know who he was now or where. He beat the drum; whatever was happening to him, he kept the rhythm. Gradually he found his way onto more gentle paths. A rider, moving at a walk, following a track, now and then bending down to look at a sign, a trail, then digging in the spurs once more – a short, sharp gallop.

He came back fast. He opened his eyes, his face brightened, relaxed, took on its usual expression. That, ladies and gentlemen, is what is known as a trance journey – this silly lecture phrase flashed through my mind. I must have looked pretty stupid. Indra got up and looked enquiringly at me. I nodded and followed him.

'Sit down there, in front of the rice bowl.'

He stood close behind me and began again, to-tock, to-tock. His drum was over me; I wasn't particularly surprised. Why not here, why not now. There had been a question. Are you afraid? The answer had been no. The reason was Indra; I trusted him, that was all. The worry of never coming back, of being stranded on the other side, evaporated the moment Indra asked me.

There was movement inside the house, everyone crowded round or stood up to get a better view; spectators were even hanging in through the windows. Shouts of joy, hoarse laughter. Suddenly something was happening in the pilgrim hostel on the eve of the great day. Tomorrow there would be prayers and sacrifices and Shakti, the power. The crowd was merry; nobody was tired, they had been sitting around together for hours, their shamans going into a trance like someone else might pop outside. That night, the attempt to drag a foreigner across into tranceland turned into a special event and a show.

I was sitting on the floor. Above my head, Indra beat the *Calling Mantra* and the only thing I could feel was a slowly, slowly widening distance to the noise around me. It broke over me, stronger now: it wants to carry me off the path, push me off the horse – let them clap, laugh, shout. The noise retreated, a breach opened, the drum forced it ajar. I moved forward, one step after another through noise and darkness. The drum beat my footsteps. I held on to Indra, he guided me. Suddenly the darkness brightened; I was in a familiar place, I saw myself wandering from room to room, through corridors and suites – a dilapidated palace, I knew it well, my resting-place of so many nights, my dream for many years. You have survived – that was the only thing I knew. Never had I met anyone else on these night-time wanders through the palace. I made myself a makeshift home underneath the high, cracked ceilings, kept finding new rooms and traces that earlier occupants had left. At one point I tried to find a way out, but the palace went on and on. I ran. The breach turned into a corridor, the drumbeat grew faster. I ran towards a gate, it was already ajar – it led out into the open, the gate was within reach. Was it my pulse beating this fast or was it the drum? My legs began to shake as I had so often seen happen to Indra. He was now beating harder, tock-to-tock, tock-to-tock, we were riding towards the gate.

What was that? A slap on my shoulder, cries of delight, the rhythmical clapping and the shouts of encouragement were all of a sudden very close again. The noise broke through. I didn't want to go back, not yet. I wanted the noise to stop, but it didn't. I opened my eyes. I felt wretched, ashamed. I was sitting on the floor in the midst of a howling crowd, the path had gone, the gate been missed, the rider torn from his horse, the people were enjoying themselves. For a second I saw Father McKenzie, his dignified priestly smile, shaking his head now. And then I saw Mai. She was here, she had kept her word. I wished I were far, far away. I wished she weren't here and weren't looking at me like this. As if she had caught me stealing furtively into her room. Not angry, astonished rather – what are you doing here?

The worst thing was that I was fêted. It had been a good night performance – the performer was offered beer, Chinese cans appearing from wicker baskets. I pushed my way outside through the crowd; Indra and Mai followed me. We walked a short distance and smoked. It was raining heavily and softly, and they made no attempt to console me. Indra just said: 'You came very close.'

I said, 'Shall we go?'

We found our camp asleep, the only light coming from the kitchen tent. We sat down and heard the rain. At some point Mai stood up and, before she went, ran her hand over my hair. And then Indra began to talk. He spoke of the myth of the mountain. How Shiva lost his companion Parvati, his great love. How she was dismembered by enemies. How the loving god, driven mad by the pain, took her in his arms and rushed over the earth, a mere wound itself, the whole world a wound. How he wailed as he had wailed before the beginning of time. How he lost Parvati, bit by bit she fell from his arms; he didn't notice in his excruciating pain. 'And wherever a bit of her fell, a shrine sprang up.' Indra pointed to where the summit lay. 'This is where her heart fell and her ...' – he searched for a polite word – 'her private parts.' A spring had flown forth from them, an impossible one, one that could only be explained by this miracle, a spring up there at the summit of the mountain. 'It never runs dry. When other springs dry up, water still drips from this one. That is where the sacrifices will take place tomorrow. Parvati wants blood. Shiva wants flowers.' For the first time that evening I saw him smile, serious Indra. 'And ganja. He likes to smoke.'

I thought that now was the moment to ask him a question that had been bothering me since I had known him. 'Indra, that photo of the Dalai Lama you always carry around with you – are you a Buddhist?'

His smile faded. He looked at me like a teacher looks at a pupil who just will not understand. 'Buddhist! Christian! That's what you want to hear? You go into your churches and temples and hope that your prayers will reach God. I see him every night. Religions are a good thing, it's good that people pray. Yes, by day I'm a Buddhist. But what I am as a shaman is far older than any religion.'

Suddenly he seemed tired, tired like an age-old man. The face of the employee from Kathmandu had disappeared and what was visible beneath it fitted what he had just said with such utter lucidity about himself. Lucidity and tiredness were two aspects of the same age. 'We are so much older than you,' he repeated. 'Your religions are simply too young for us.' He fiddled with his necklace. 'Have you ever heard of Rudra?'

'The old god, the howler.'

'The fruit my necklace is made of is called rudraksha, which means Rudra's tears. I wear Shiva's tears when I go to him.'

He explained to me the meaning of the number of fruits hanging from the necklace and of the different grooves in their nutty surfaces, but I was too tired to follow what he was saying. He didn't care, he carried on talking, he talked to himself. 'We men of today, we fight with ghosts. The ancients fought with gods. So much we are no longer capable of. So much is lost.'

That was the last thing I heard. I stretched out and fell asleep.

⤙

I had somehow made it to my tent. The kitchen boy was already scratching on the tarpaulin and offering his morning greetings. 'Morning, sir. Morning tea.' I opened the zip as always; friendly as always, he handed me the steaming tea, and as always I remained in the tent for a few minutes and warmed myself up with the hot bowl. It was now bitterly cold in the morning. The warmth of the valleys and woods lay far below us, but on the other hand there were no leeches here.

I crawled out of the tent. The camp was already awake, the shamans had gone to carry out their ritual cleansing at one particular spring. Something was different from usual and at the very moment I had the thought, I saw it – the sky. My God, it was clearing up. Fog and clouds, the thick shrouds that had hidden the view from us for so long, were evaporating. The sun broke through red between the banks of cloud. Could it be true that, today of all days, it should vanquish the sea of fog? Mohan was in the best possible mood. For him, it was the glorious triumph of everything he believed in. 'I promised you, didn't I?' he said. 'The shamans have been drumming all these days for this. Now see for yourself!'

He was right – the sun was getting stronger by the minute. The milky morning sky was turning blue. Spellbound at this spectacle, we stood on the secondary summit and watched as the veils were simply drawn aside in the time it takes to drink a cup of tea. *Morning, sir. Morning sun.* Facing east, we watched the sunrise, shabby cotton clothes turning red, faces glowing. I read people's thoughts, it wasn't hard. So many blessings. Such was Shiva's and the goddess's love for us that today they rip open the sky for us. What a blessed day.

Then everyone went uphill, shoulder to shoulder; the pilgrim hostel was empty once more, the iron bridge above us squeaked and swayed under the unaccustomed weight. I was soon at the top; for the second time in a few hours, I saw Shiva's plateau. How different from yesterday evening. Now the plateau lay in the light, and at its feet lay the world.

The summit dropped off steeply on all sides. The mountains of the Himalayas were arranged in a full 360-degree panorama, for this one moment only. Their majesties glittered crystalline, their white slopes sent down millions of little lightning bolts. Then I heard singing. From the valleys below us, almost entire villages approached, singing as they came along all seven paths to the summit, following their shamans. And these were not city-dwellers like Indra, they were wild figures in ripped trousers and dirty shirts, they came barefoot or in Chinese flip-flops, their matted hair stood on end and, for lack of an intact feather crown, they had stuck a few tattered feathers into it; their drums could hardly be called drums anymore, so flat and bent and shapeless had they become from long years of use.

I was now standing on the plateau at which I had taken a first look yesterday, and caught sight of a corrugated iron shack, no bigger than a building site toilet and so plain and windowless that I had overlooked it in the dusk. It was a prayer hut, open only on the plateau side. An old man, a skinny Brahman, sat inside it in the yoga position. He was reading the *Bhagavadgītā* and sought to calm his mind and ignore the wild, bloody, pre-Vedic goings-on. The shamans and their followers, for their part, ignored the Brahman; they paid him no heed. This was their day, not his. This was their mountain, not some old Hindu philosopher's. He sat there like a stone in a river, washed by wave after wave. It was just as Indra had said. That man was praying. That man was searching for God in the book. They were running to the goddess of the mountain and throwing themselves at her breast.

I let myself be pulled along by the crowd and ended up in front of the rusty trident mountain that I had seen yesterday in silhouette. Children were clambering about on the hill of rust and iron, and trying to pick up coins that the faithful had flung onto the iron heap along with new tridents, flowers, rice, maize and ganja weed. I was witness to devout prayers to Shiva's godhead – and to the great respect being paid to the little red king. When he appeared beside the hill of tridents, a half-circle immediately formed around him.

'We bring you milk from the white cow,' he prayed. 'Milk from the white goat, milk from the white frog, as you requested.' And then, in comical desperation at the unfulfilled third oath, once more: 'We only have cows and goats, as you know; you know our heart and our need. So give us what we lack, that is our request. Give us water, give us crops, give us strength.' The slightly built old man threw himself on top of the iron straw, embraced the rust and the lances, paused, finally let go, realized that he couldn't stay here, took a step backwards, was caught up by his own, and swept away.

His prayer had been about what was possible and what was impossible for men, about the humility of kings. The absurd white frog's milk was the imperfect nature of man, the power beyond his power, the missing link that would make him perfect – it was what God must add. However, this was not the time for theology and certainly not the place. The crowd circled its way forward across the plateau. I was forced out and found myself beside an iron fence; it was said that the government had had it put up to prevent anyone falling to his death from the plateau during fights between opposing villages and shamans as must have happened in the past. The fence was a wobbly little railing, a thin iron rod on equally thin and wobbly posts that ran around the plateau at hip height; it wouldn't prevent anything. I held on to it anyway, allowed the crowd to pass by, turned my back, just stood there and looked at the mountains. I would have had to fly to see them. Shiva Airways, I thought, the doctor, our youthful anticipation about the adventure awaiting us. Now I was here. Where was he? I had lost sight of him early that day.

I pushed my way into the circling crowd, followed the smell of blood that hung in the air, and the crowd pushed me onwards, onwards, into the furthest corner of the plateau, in front of the sacrificial shrine to the goddess. It was an unremarkable stone, shapeless and completely covered in blood. Parvati's private parts, her inexhaustible spring, contrary to all logic. There were goats there, their bleating was in the air, it was their blood being spilt. They were led forward, one after the other; seconds later, with slit throats, they leapt away, to die after a few final trembling steps. One goat stood tied to a stake there and grazed. There was something almost manic about the way it pulled up the grass and devoured it as if it could put off its imminent death by eating, by plucking, furious at the grass that would live while its warm blood ran over the goddess's pudenda.

One man brought white doves, another brought chickens. The knife worked from sunrise until noon, then Parvati had drunk enough. Enough victims, enough prayers, enough Amrit had dripped down from the sky, enough Shakti had been lavishly distributed. Enough – the gods drew a veil over their magnificence. The Himalayas disappeared again as fast as they had revealed themselves that morning and the plateau now emptied just as fast.

Smoke was already rising from fires on the slopes of the secondary summit. The aromas of the sacrificed animals being roasted over them filled the air, which had by now turned cooler. Everyone ate their fill and drank and dozed on the hard grass, then, after scrutinizing the sky and the clouds closing in from all sides, the entire sacrificial gathering set off. Soon a great many shaman columns were going back down into the valley by the seven paths. The wind swirled up scraps and ash, still warm, but the summit was empty, the meeting of men and gods over for this year.

We too set off. We took a different, particularly steep but shorter route. After a two-day march, we saw the track in the valley bottom where our bus would pick us up. The last few kilometres, we didn't walk downhill, we skipped and ran. When I reached the track, my eyes alighted on a stone. I sat down on it. I sat on it as if I had merged with it, for hours. If I stood up, the stone would stand up too.

At some point the bus came; there had been another landslide or something, I couldn't muster any interest in it. The return journey was wonderful, being driven and rocked over the passes. It was night by the time we drove into a beeping, clattering, screeching hell. I was surprised and couldn't believe that this was the same city from which we had set out ten days earlier; I didn't recognize Kathmandu. The thick clouds of exhaust fumes, the soot on everything, the noise. As a cure, the doctor suggested we go to a Tsarist restaurant, where we were served by Russians in pre-revolutionary uniforms.

The next evening we organized a leaving party for our sherpas. All the ordeals we had come through left us, all the dangers we had endured faded into memory and memory into anecdotes – told, admired, embellished, seasoned, sugared a-plenty. It was a joyful party. The old shaman and his wife had driven to Kathmandu with us and were there with us that evening as well. I wanted to give him a present and, since I had nothing else I could have given him, I took off my deck shoes – they were by now as shapeless as old shaman drums from all the trekking through mountain torrents and rain – and handed them to him. The red king's feet were much smaller than mine, but did that really matter? How could anyone be fussy on an evening like this?

Mai had come to the leaving party too. We said hello from a distance, but I couldn't stand it at the table for long. I know as little today as I did at the time about what drove me to do it; I saw myself get up, go over to her, fall to my knees, take her hand and urgently ask her to be my wife. To my dismay, she turned me down. She did so in a friendly, sensitive, almost loving manner. I repeated my request in desperation. With utter patience, she explained to me that it was not possible. Mai was married, as I had in fact known but forgotten as I forgot myself. The party continued, no one took any notice of what was happening at Mai's table. My head was lying in her lap. Only gradually did I calm down.

The memories of her and me are like a handful of blurred red-tinged photos laid out side by side. The last picture showed the doctor with a sympathetic grin on his bearded face. 'This always happens,' I heard him say. 'You fall in love with the first woman shaman you meet. And it doesn't matter if she's beautiful or not, whether she's young or old.'

～

Early light is dawning at the window. Something hard is pressing against my temple – I must have fallen asleep on Shiva's tears. On the table is the silver tea bowl. The relief decoration running round it shows dragons and Himalayan peaks and, floating above them, tiny clouds and the blue Garuda that doesn't feature in any zoological textbook. 'From Tibet,' said the man in Kathmandu who sold me the bowl. 'From a high lama. Pure silver, sir.' I sometimes drink tea out of it. The tea is bitter and cold now. I write the final sentence.

The God of Roppongi

How much further to Tokyo? I hadn't been able to sleep all flight and was afraid this might continue. Tokyo would be a squidgy sandwich of waiting. A stopover. A night crammed between two half-eaten days, today and tomorrow, then the onward flight. I tried to concentrate on the screen on the back of the seat in front of me, on the map which showed half the world and us, a dot creeping towards morning. Suddenly, as the Airbus flew along the edge of the Eurasian night and the White Sea, a long forgotten event came to my mind. It had taken place in the other hemisphere, on a trip to America in the early eighties, in a hotel in New Hampshire.

I had received an unusual request to share my room with a guest, a 'gentleman from Tokyo', only for a couple of nights, an unfortunate bottleneck, they would bring in a second bed, 'we're so sorry'. Whether this was true or whether the hotel manager was a war veteran who just thought it would make a grim joke to shut the former Axis powers up together in a relatively small room – I didn't think about it much at the time. The young German abroad immediately agreed, keen to appear impeccably polite, come what may. I went to bed late that evening though, without turning the light on again.

The new day in New Hampshire began – it was just dawning – with a quiet, shrill noise. I opened my eyes; the gentleman from Tokyo had leapt up from his sleeping position, throwing the linen sheet to one side as he did so. He was sitting bolt upright in bed, his legs at right angles to his trunk. He did this so he could bow. Already wide awake, he wished me a firm 'Good morning!' while bowing in typical fashion. It was so precise it looked like an early morning exercise; these polite gymnastics lasted for a minute, then he jumped to his feet. Now, though, the fun was over and I was deeply ashamed. The gentleman from Tokyo gave me a present. An apple. Flabbergasted, I accepted it and thanked him awkwardly; and the next morning the same thing happened again: he gave me a present; and again on the third morning. Following the apple, the second morning gift was a packet of Japanese cigarettes and the third a little book in English about Zen. I felt like an oaf – the emotionally stunted Parsifal who has no idea how to be polite. What should I do? A cigarette swap with the half-full, squashed packet I had left? Some pine cones I'd collected? I had nothing on me with which I might have reciprocated his gifts, and didn't know how to get hold of anything – the hotel lay all on its own out in the forests of New Hampshire.

In the end, my first ever Japanese disappeared from my hotel room and my life, but not from me. He defined how I saw his country. If the hotel manager's intention had indeed been to punish the Axis through unbearable closeness, then he achieved quite the opposite.

Later, I realized what had happened to me. It had been summer, the season of presents in Japan. This information only increased my astonishment. A country with a season of gifts. And not just one evening of present-giving, when life's usual course was suspended for two hours, only to resume even more frenetically – no, an entire season. My room-mate could easily have skipped this Japanese custom on his travels; it was unknown in America and no one would have noticed. He wouldn't have considered it. For whoever he met, even if it was a stranger lying in the next bed one morning, he had gifts in his big suitcase. Light gifts, as light as watercolours. If you laid them out next to each other, they formed a pictogram: Apple. Smoke. Zen. Eat an apple. Blow cigarette smoke into the air and contemplate the shapes it makes. Exercise. It was all so simple, so logical, so beautiful – and so odd. You could take the three objects literally of course: Apple smoke Zen. And if you read it backwards it became: Zen smoke apple. So that was what Japan was like. Simply beautifully odd.

～

As we fell down through the sky and glided and bumped through mountains of cloud, a voice said that we had already left our cruising altitude – but Tokyo just wouldn't appear. I saw something through my porthole just seconds before we touched down on the runway. Planes in their docking positions at Terminal 1. The markings on the wet asphalt. Special vehicles, which looked like they'd been built by children, doing strange manoeuvres. Men in red and yellow helmets making signals with their arms that were no less strange. Narita in the rain. Welcome to Tokyo, the voice said.

A taxi stood in front of the airport. The driver got out, held up his left hand to protect his head in a shielding but pointless gesture to keep the rain off his elaborately combed hair, barely listened as I called out the hotel address to him, and gestured silently with his right hand: Just get in.

To my surprise, I knew the city he drove me into. Not one house looked older than me, not one seemed anything other than functional. Tokyo left my eyes hungry, let the greedy gaze of the foreigner seeking the foreign slide off it. And it wasn't in the mood to make life easy for me. No service, said my telephone. Neither my credit card nor my languages were of any service either. No reception. No money. No answer to my requests for directions. Even my sense of direction let me down. Tokyo's streets, apart from the main ones, don't have names, and its houses don't have numbers; every guidebook mentioned this, but that was no help. I threw the guidebook away and bought an umbrella. Everyone here carried one. The season of gifts was also that of rain. The young saleswoman didn't look at me. She had a face made of white porcelain and she gave me the umbrella like an auxiliary nurse doling out bread rations. I walked through Tokyo under my new umbrella, walked and walked through the rain, cloaked in total absence. No one could have been more invisible that day.

I was actually tired, but I didn't want to go to bed and miss out on Tokyo. Another 39 hours. When the rain started falling more heavily, I decided to go into a café. It was called Salon Vert, with white-and-green awnings and wicker chairs. I had spotted it from a distance; it was near the Ueno Park, which I had been circling for a while. White-and-green striped awnings and warm-brown-coloured wicker chairs – I was longing for just this type of place right now. I was drenched when I reached it. I should have known that I was chasing a nostalgic whim. Awnings and wicker chairs? But those familiar signs didn't mean the same here. Salon Vert was a cafeteria.

I gave up. At the hotel, I dropped onto the bed and into a deep sleep from which I only awoke hours later.

❦

How quiet it was. The rain had stopped and left behind only a memory – a drizzle as fine as dust. I went out into the evening and walked through lanes that had been deserted during the day; now the shutters were pushed up and printed material and lanterns hung everywhere, and it smelt of beer and fish. In narrow, sometimes makeshift-looking houses, bars, cafés and restaurants were opening. These labyrinthine lanes lay between main roads or in the shadow of skyscrapers, like villages between two rivers or at the foot of a mountain – urban villages with no livestock, no fields, no name. Apple. Cigarettes. Zen. It was back. So this was where the gifts had come from. This is where they belonged.

I was hungry and went into a sushi bar. Behind the counter, two men – a gaunt old man who was constantly cleaning a big knife every time he used it, and a fat young man who assisted him. The old man called out, very loudly, to me as I entered and guided me towards a free seat at his counter. I heard those loud calls many more times that evening. It was a ritual. The master shouted something loudly to his assistant standing next to him, who answered just as loudly: 'Hai! Hai!' The knife was the old man's all-purpose tool: it cut, it skinned, it filleted, it clove big lumps in half and carried out the tiniest of operations. His hands had reached that supreme level of skill at which the fingers know by themselves what to do and do it quickly and nimbly, picking out the last few fish bones, shaping, kneading, sprinkling, basting and serving in seconds, while their master chatted to the guests and had his mind on other things.

The customer next to me was eating and drinking sake, purring with contentment. The prevailing atmosphere was of something like cordial coolness. The dishes, the knife, the spirits you drank with your fish – none of this was warm. What was warm were the shouts, the voices, the patrons' feeling of being well looked after under the old man's watchful gaze. His eyes said: I know what you need, I know better than you do. I needed something warm and he noticed. He shouted something to his staff. Tea arrived. A large mug of green tea.

I left, roamed about for a while and stopped in front of a café that somehow attracted me, maybe it was the landlady, a good-looking, middle-aged Japanese woman, whose face was not made of porcelain. She noticed my indecision and invited me to take a seat. I decided on the left-hand of the only two tables, ordered and listened to conversations at the bar which I didn't understand and which lulled me to sleep like a pleasant jazz tune. It was past midnight. It wouldn't have taken much for me to fall asleep at my table. Then a petite old woman came in, meticulously dressed and made-up. The landlady, who had not been particularly formal up to this point, greeted her in traditional manner with a bow and served her a Martini, although the old lady had not yet said what she wanted. She only took small sips of it. There was an aura of respect about her; the lively conversation at the bar continued at a slightly lower volume. After ten minutes she stood up and left, faultlessly accompanied over the threshold by the landlady, who watched her walk away along the dark lane. When the landlady came back, she stopped at my table.

'You're wondering who she is?'

'What makes you think that?'

'Every new customer wonders who she is.'

'And who is she?'

'She was a geisha. She always had sumo wrestlers. The way things work: you get recommended.' She said that an American reporter used to come to the café every day for months around this time to persuade the old lady to put her memoirs down on paper with his help. 'She just laughed. All those men, she said, so many memories. They keep me warm now in my old age. What would I have left if I gave them away? The reporter was literally in despair. He couldn't understand. He was convinced that he was making her a valuable gift with her memoirs.'

At first light I got up, left the hotel and once again – how quiet it was! Dew lay on the new day. In the parks, elderly gentleman had turned up for early morning exercise; in front of the shops, employees in black trousers and white shirts assembled for morning roll-call. Tokyo was springing to life, but the silence held. Even if the streets were livelier and the underground fuller, no one ran, no one shouted, no one jostled or bothered anyone else. Space was at a premium, and people acted like the houses, the skyscrapers and the villages between them: they nimbly made way, using every nook and cranny. Big city courtesy that cannot be dictated and only comes about with long practice.

Courtesy was the key. In the lobby of an office block, I watched employees going off for their lunch break – but I watched the reception staff even more closely. A dozen of them in uniform, bowing deeply to every new crowd of employees that stepped out of the lift, for minutes on end, probably for hours on end, ceaselessly. And even the loud shouts of the human shepherds that appeared during rush hour in the underground stations and pushed passengers into the carriages until not one more would fit sounded more like the ritual whistles with which village boys drive the herds homewards in the evening than bellowed commands.

Elderly couples were the epitome of this peacefulness. Old ramblers, I thought to myself, because that's what they looked like. Their olive- or sand-coloured hiking outfits, all their functional clothing, the way they moved in groups. And the hats. Almost all of them wore shapeless, slightly crumpled sunhats like the ones you see at the beach or on long-distance footpaths. Their demureness too. These couples were not modern old people, they didn't go in for storming up mountains; they walked long distances, they went their way. Maybe they'd been lovers, maybe they still were. They hid it. That wasn't proper behaviour in the street and they concealed it behind their walking paraphernalia.

Companions – that was how they dressed, that was how they acted. Life companions – the awkward, hesitant euphemism from back home sounded right here. It defined the situation the way it was and could not be otherwise.

It was a hot day. Tokyo steamed in the humid heat, but the small valley I had discovered cooled me down, a spacious, slightly lower square in the middle of an elegant area at the foot of skyscrapers whose lower floors were devoted to luxury and pleasure, and whose upper floors were given over to business. Along one side of the square, not far above our heads, ran an expressway. On another, artificial waterfalls burbled, lots of them. The rain had retreated over the sea for a few hours, but the waterfalls imitated its roar and kept its memory alive – a rain shrine.

In front of it men stood smoking in black suits – the scrupulously observed uniform of managers and executives. They smoked in silence and seemed to be listening to the falling water, but their expressions were empty, as empty as the faces of people asleep on the underground. This ability to catnap in public, to empty oneself for the time it takes to smoke a cigarette, contributed greatly to Tokyo's silence. The cheap concrete slabs we were standing on, thick with stamped-out cigarette butts, the caretaker who would appear from time to time to sweep them away with his besom – this was the smokers' corner of the city. A couple more drags, then the silent smokers would once again ride up into their office blocks, which towered so proudly and spotlessly against the sun. Yes, they were the pride of Tokyo, these high-rise buildings. Gigantic sculptures of stone, steel and glass, some of them rounded, others tapered in the middle; they didn't surround us like buildings do, they displayed themselves like works of art.

The midday heat drove me into the parks. In the Yasukuni shrine, I settled down on a low wall for a rest, but the park-keeper pointed me to the benches for this purpose beneath the trees. No sooner had I sat down than I felt a gentle blow on my chest. A red stain appeared on my white shirt, as if from some tiny projectile. Just a drop from the beak of a bird that was pecking at red berries in the tree above me. I walked on and, when I felt tired, abandoned myself to the nearest underground. I came out at the foot of what seemed to me a particularly mighty, towering chain of skyscrapers. That's how it was: you were invited to enter. The top floor of the Roppongi Hills Mori Tower, a sign said, had panoramic glass and offered magnificent views of Tokyo – 360 degrees from 240 metres up.

I took the lift and walked up to the wall of glass. Tokyo was spread out beneath me, and at last the sultry heat broke. A thunderstorm beat down directly overhead. The streaks of lightning, wild and pale, seemed to come from the skyscrapers themselves, one tree of lightning, one fiery stem after another. But the silence held. The world outside was totally, utterly soundless. None of the crashing on the other side of the glass, however violent, could be heard inside. It was a picture, nothing more. The thunder was just as inaudible as the traffic far below, as the planes and helicopters that occasionally shot out of the clouds. The city was never-ending; it merged into the rainy mist on all sides. Individual areas would stand out dimly for a few minutes in the sunlight until it faded again. Other areas were in gloom, a blackish grey. Night had already settled over the lowlands.

Now I saw it: Tokyo was a city without roofs. The city came to such an abrupt vertical halt that it looked as if building had just stopped one day. Its houses and skyscrapers had no goal, no roof – they just broke off. Some owners obviously had a vague sense that there was something slightly wrong and had put some flower boxes on the platforms. But most of these surfaces were covered in all kinds of structures, pipes and technical tentacles as well as plugs and cables, and all of them looked as if they had been pulled out. Red marker lights flashed over the city as if announcing some power failure. If you had binoculars, you could make out shrines that still had roofs. Magnificent, overhanging roofs culminating in tips that bent skywards. Through the long years when man was unable to see his world from above – a privilege of the gods – he had gone to great lengths to build splendid and lavishly ornate roofs such as these. Now that it was so simple for him to study his creations from above, he didn't care. I had had sunglasses made for moments like these; through them everything looked bathed in golden light. I put them on and Tokyo glowed.

I soon took them off again to study an exceptionally well-dressed couple. She was wearing a traditional kimono and moved perfectly in it, upright, taking small steps, he a matt black bespoke suit whose sharply cut lines were emphasized by a sharply folded, white dress handkerchief. I'd taken my eyes off the panorama; the glass gallery was but the showcase for the real attraction up here. The highest summit, the centre of the 53rd floor, had been chosen to exhibit art – an art gallery which I was now entering and the couple were leaving.

You don't stare at people in Tokyo. You don't do it anywhere, but in Tokyo no one does it. And yet I couldn't take my eyes off the two of them. I noticed that he'd noticed and, to avert the resulting embarrassment, he made a slight bow and handed me the catalogue he had been carrying under his arm. I took it, and a somewhat forced conversation began.

'We love art,' he said, and his wife in her wonderful kimono smiled politely.

'Are you collectors?' I asked.

'Oh yes,' he said absentmindedly, 'we are collectors.' It was up to me to bring the conversation to an end. I bowed, muttering some words of thanks, but when I tried to give him back the catalogue, which I'd been holding like a roof tile, he unexpectedly carried on talking.

'We do business,' he said, suddenly serious, 'good business. And what do we do then? More good business.' An almost desperate expression came over his somewhat wilted but nevertheless manly face. 'Why? If we have no answer to that, then we are mere apes. Very clever apes.'

His wife looked at him with affection but also some disquiet. She found the situation inappropriate. She wanted to leave.

'You have seen the panorama,' he continued, 'the skyscrapers?'

Hastily I nodded.

'Tokyo is a sculpture, it is young, it is our creation, and the creating goes on. Oh, forgive me, I am detaining you. Please go, please go, have a look at everything. It is only as artists that we are free.' He bowed and was gone. And I stood there, still holding the catalogue in both hands, his gift. Once more it was summer, the time of gifts, and once again I was the idiot. I went into the exhibition.

He had spoken of art like a religion. And indeed there was a good deal of taboo and transcendence. There were signs in front of the exhibits that read 'Please don't touch the art!' The visitors walked around the untouchable works of art, their audio-guides to their ears. There were the believers, sunk in contemplation, silent worship even, and believers to whom the pious gestures came easily by force of habit. There were the dutiful, who came because it was expected of them, and the absentminded, who were perhaps seeking – had always sought – something in art, but weren't quite able to concentrate on it at the moment, as they had been unable to concentrate earlier and indeed would be unable to do so in the future too. And finally there were the art theologians, with an eye for the subtleties of quotations and rituals, unbelieving but well-versed. In short, it was just like being in a real church.

However, I had been making these observations in the side chapels. At the front, where the believers thronged, must be the magnetic centre, the holy of holies. What could it be? One could discount this being some abstract flight of fancy; the idea of putting art at the top of one of the city's highest towers – the cult of all the men in the black suits – was too deliberate for that. No, it had to be an image. A figure.

It was an animal. Two animals. Mother and calf. Their faces were cut cleanly lengthways and so were their whole bodies. I pushed my way through the crowd and stood in front of the sawn-up calf and the sawn-up cow by the artist Damien Hirst – so this was it. The cleanly executed joke of a tyrannical child. Look what I can do! I'm just going to do it, and I'm going to do it now. There was a note on the wall with the usual litany about art designed to provoke and set you thinking. Someone went 'Moo!' and we left. On a high table on the way out lay an apple with a bite out of it and a half-smoked cigarette. I put the catalogue down beside them. Apple smoke art.

Then I was standing at the foot of the tower or, should I say, of the temple mountain? Rain streamed down my face. I had seen the highest and the holiest – what did I have to fear? I looked at my watch. It was time to fly.

Shangri-La

We are gripped by a special kind of tension when we travel, when we penetrate into remote areas. We look and look, drive, drive and almost stop talking. The way we see causes the talk that usually helps us cope to cease. Nothing but the present. Whatever else we have been pales into insignificance, as in love, as in battle. We wander through foreign terrain – extreme vigilance. But here it is not because of ambushes, it is because of whatever appears in the corner of our eye or on the horizon at a particular moment. The moment is an elusive prey and the horizon always wherever we are not. An insatiable hunt, and we know it. The hunt is just a pretext. All that counts is the hour at the edge of the clearing.

Somewhere out there, where Burma, Tibet and the southern Chinese province of Yunnan tail out in craggy borderlands, I followed a sidearm of the Yangtze into the mountains from where it came. The olive-green water had – at least from a distance – the consistency of gelatine. I was following this river because of a word, a name. Up there, where the air grew thin, at an altitude of about 3,500 metres, my map indicated a place I had thought existed only in legends and films – Shangri-La.

We were now a good 3,000 metres up. When I leaned out of the window and looked into the chasm beside the road, I could see the river becoming younger and younger. It was a different river up here. No longer a wide, gelatinous stream; a torrent that foamed up and squeezed itself into an ever-narrowing gorge and forced its way through stone and rock. The road had been dynamited out of the mountain and wound upwards towards the top of the pass; the driver drew an astounding performance from the Chinese minibus.

Sometimes a village would cling onto the mountain

like a stone nest. Among the rocks grew yellow and purple flowers, in the pine trees bright-green shoots; the icy peaks were shrouded in cloud. Once, the road widened out into an inhabited high valley that was cultivated right up to the edge of the mountains. Farmers had harnessed yaks and were ploughing the soil. I soon gave up counting the stupas and prayer flags – there were too many of them. If I had asked the Chinese driver whether we were still in China or already in Tibet, it would have been contentious, even though the answer was obvious. Light rain was falling when we reached the top of the pass; a large stupa, pine trees and prayer flags here too. The army post let us through. I got up and walked down the slope – the number of breaths required to take a few steps had doubled.

Soon after the pass the countryside changed again, we now arrived at a high plateau. Everything widened and cleared, the colours and shapes; we emerged from the deep, out of chasms and, for the first time, saw where we were. The roof of the world – the word became reality. The high plateau was Mongolian green, surrounded by far-off mountain ranges, whose highest peaks lay in eternal snow. Tibetan farms with their trapezoid windows, blue-red cornices and overhanging shingle roofs, black from the weather and weighed down with white stones that looked like mushrooms, were scattered across the grassy steppe. There were wooden racks as tall as houses; they reminded you of the skeletons of gigantic, extinct animals. If we hadn't been in Tibet, I might have thought that Max Ernst had spent some time here. During the short summers, said the driver when I asked him about them, hay and straw were dried on the racks.

We reached Shangri-La before nightfall. I felt an expectant atmosphere about the place, a sense of promise I couldn't quite explain. It must have been the women in traditional Tibetan costume, hurrying home as though they still had important things to prepare for the great day. It must have been the cleanliness of the squares and lanes too, and the sounds of carpentry coming from here and there. All the houses in Shangri-La were traditional wood buildings and their façades ornately carved, and in the twilight they were still being hammered and sawed at, as if Shangri-La had to be completed by next morning. A bar-owner was just nailing a sign above his door: 'Shangri-La Feeling Bar'. And it must have been because of the light. The night didn't fall like a black cushion suffocating everything – the day took its time leaving. The plain had long been dark, but the white peaks of Shangri-La still stood in the last light.

I found a hotel, a particularly splendid, new wooden construction, then I went to eat. I chose Tibetan-style salted and dried yak meat, roasted wild flowers and tea. The waiter had warned me that the meat was old and very salty, and suggested I eat a more classically cooked yak dish, but my yak was exactly right. Salty, without being over-salted. Dry, crunchy in parts and tender too. The roasted flowers, a large plateful of them, looked like a pile of fried mountain insects; I had the feeling I was eating something very wild. One thing intrigued me: everything here was so beautiful, so perfect, so pukka. On the way to Shangri-La, I had come through many a rough place and sat at tables whose faded plastic cloths were worn out and stained with the remains of other guests' meals, and the dishes set down on these tables had been very Tibetan or very Chinese, in any case not meant to appeal to a foreign stomach or eye.

I had seen a glow over Shangri-La in the twilight. Now I walked through the town – many shops had opened, shops selling furs, Tibetan silver jewellery and Tibetan medicine, tankas and Bodhisattvas and tea, genuine and fake antiques, in short everything that a traveller might like to look at and buy as he strolls through the streets after a good meal. I had eaten well, was strolling about, noticed how its mood was working on me, and bought a fur hat. That would be enough, for a while at least. Then I walked towards the dazzling golden glow.

It was a lamaic temple and it was – I could see this even in the dark – brand new. And what had shone out into the plain was its prayer wheel. I had often seen this type of prayer device, small and large spinning drums that rattled loudly or softly; believers walked past them and kept them moving to multiply their prayers and increase their impact. But the one that towered up here was like no other. The prayer wheel at Shangri-La was the size of a Berlin water tower. A huge golden drum above the promised town, impossible to overlook by day and also by night, for it was floodlit. I approached it and recognized a socialist realist-style relief running round the bottom of it. Every national minority in the province, all holding hands in harmony. Probably the largest prayer wheel in the world was a state wheel, activated by an aluminium hand-rail as thick as my arm. There were Chinese tourists there, young and elderly couples. The men got down to pushing the wheel, making a show of it while their wives took photos of them. All the men were wearing what looked like cowboy hats. Obviously an obligatory souvenir. They were piled high in the shops of Shangri-La.

On my way through the dark lanes I passed a bar. Sexy Yeti was its name and there were unmistakable signs that it belonged to an Englishman. The photo of the Queen in an Indian silver frame among the whisky bottles standing on the shelf, a jar of biscuits, a few copies of the *Spectator* from the previous year on the end of the bar and above all the landlord himself, a bony, sandy-haired chap of about 50 with a Mancunian accent.

The patrons were mostly young Tibetans, sitting with beer and tea at ironwork tables with charcoal burners in them; in some of them, embers still glimmered under the ashes, and when someone poked them, they glowed bright red. The dark wooden floor was covered with the light-coloured shells of sunflower seeds. There was a notice listing what the Sexy Yeti had to offer: Sexy Drinks, Sexy Pizza, Western Breakfast. Two dozen books stood on a plank, and among them was, of course, a particularly dog-eared copy of *Lost Horizon*. One of the landlord's countrymen, who had taken the pen name James Hilton, picked up the legend of Shangri-La – the paradise beyond Tibet's eight-thousanders – somewhere around 1930, and turned it into a novel, giving the West's dream of Tibet an old name and cloaking it in a new, more adventurous version that had the advantage of being set in the author's own time. A propeller plane goes missing in the Himalayas, its passenger a senior diplomat who later turns up somewhere completely different and tells of the fabulous place beyond the deserts of ice. An account that remains suspect and fragmentary, and yet ... it contains some surprising clues; the legend of Shangri-La lives on.

'Cigars had burned low ...' Thus begins *Lost Horizon*, at a dinner attended by a few gentlemen in Berlin, at the Tempelhof airport casino. With the four men's memories of India – exhaled and evoked.

'Staying for long, sir?' The landlord's question fetched me back from my thoughts.

'I will leave tomorrow.'

He nodded. 'Takes time, takes time.'

'What do you mean?'

'The whole Shangri-La thing, man. It's getting started, but only Chinese up to now. You're the first white tourist. Where are you all? Everything's ready. I'm waiting.' He crossed his arms and smiled a proprietorial smile. 'Come on, let's have a drink.' He poured us two malts, an unpleasant situation because I can't stand whisky. 'Cheers!' – 'Cheers!' He was too distracted to notice that I was only sipping at it. 'The Shangri-La thing, man!'

After a while, he poured himself another one. He began to talk. About how the government had come up with the idea of creating a model Tibet. A No Problem Tibet. About how they had decided on this previously unknown area, an old Tibetan town beyond the mountains, located on a Mongolian green high plateau, a town entirely built and carved out of wood, surrounded by snowy peaks, which lay bathed in the last light when the day had already moved on far to the west.

'There were only two things missing,' the landlord continued. 'A great temple and a great name. Especially the name.' He pulled Hilton's novel off the shelf and waved it at me like the Great Leader waving his Red Book at the masses. 'Shangri-La – a fantastic name, you've got to admit.'

I asked him if he was the one who'd suggested it to the Chinese. He shrugged, but there wasn't actually any doubt. Then he changed the subject. 'Been to the new temple up there?'

'Yes, I've just got back.'

He nodded, lost in thought. I put down some money. We said goodbye wordlessly as I left, like old acquaintances.

～

On the short stretch to the hotel I met three army patrols, each of six men marching along beside their officer in the grass-green uniforms of the People's Liberation Army. The colour of grass in midsummer before it goes yellow. I prolonged my walk, headed out onto the high plateau, towards where the snowy peaks lay in the moonlight. I had been walking for a while when something dark rose up out of the grassland; a fire was burning. I walked towards it and reached an army camp. The dark shapes were long rows of patrol tents and troop transporters; soldiers were warming themselves with their tea-cups around the bivouac and clicking their heels to keep the night's frost at bay. Before the guards could notice me, I turned round and gave the camp a wide berth.

I could see it from afar. And from afar I saw the town with the golden water tower and the snow-covered peaks. I hadn't made it to Shangri-La. But I was very far from everything. And that's something.